Endless lists of things you're supposed
to be happy about.
People who think they've learned everything
they need to know in kindergarten.
Mondays.
Pens that run out of ink in mid-check.
Pens that leak oozy blobs onto greeting
cards.
Back-to-back commercials for diet centers
and pizza delivery.
Leaving an age bracket.
Middle seats on airplanes.
Free opera tickets.
Men who say they want a woman who looks
natural and then ogle all the women
in makeup.
Babies screaming in restaurants.
Waiters with bad colds.
Very. slow. elevators.
Speed bumps.
Warm beer.
Bed partners with Ninja-weapon toenails.
Repairmen who can't keep their pants up.
Men who choreograph five long hairs over

continued on page 13

1,000,001 THINGS THAT MAKE YOU CRABBY

THE OFFICIAL CHECKLIST FOR
COMPLAINERS, RANT 'N' RAVERS
& BELLYACHERS.
AND EVERYBODY ELSE.

BY NATALIE WINDSOR
ILLUSTRATED BY JOE AZAR

CORKSCREW PRESS
LOS ANGELES

CorkScrew Press
4470-107 Sunset Blvd., Suite 234
Los Angeles, CA 90027

Distributed in Canada by Firefly Books, Ltd.,
250 Sparks Ave., Willowdale, Ontario M2H 2S4

ISBN 0-944042-06-6
Library of Congress Number 91-071052

Printed in the U.S.A.
First printing April 1991

10 9 8 7 6 5 4 3 2 1

"It does not matter what is done to us. What matters is what we do with what is done to us."

—*Sartre*

Special Thanks for
Love, Support and/or Assistance

Patti Putnicki, Michele Milder,
Bruce Gossard & Mary Lyon,
Mark "Blacksheep" Schwartz, Kathy
Walker, Rabbi Michael Signer,
Jonathan Omer-man, Kathi Sharpe-Ross,
Isosceles the Philosopher, Rich Lippman,
Joe Azar and my Mom, Ruth,
whom I've been making
crabby for years.

CorkScrew Press Thanks

Peggy Richter, Eric Skopec, Bob
Mullin, Bob Spar, Ken Niles, Ad
Infinitum, Mark Jansen, Bill Cates,
Randy Anderson, Dennis Goris, Ron
Pottle, CrabEnders, Inc., Ro & Shel,
Eric Clapton and Jack Daniels.

Consider this book a purgative for your soul. It's cathartic.

If you're counting crabbies, start with: *People who throw around ten-dollar words.* But add: *People obsessed with counting things.*

My dear editor and publisher Rich Lippman says I'm such an optimist, I'm perfect to write a book about what burns your burgers. In his twisted way, he's right. Somehow, endless lists of pet peeves become funny instead of irritating. They seem to pull reactions out of people who never express feelings about *anything*. A paper clip and highlighter also make this book into a conversational marital aid.

If I missed your personal saddle burr, don't get bent; just turn to page 173 and vent your spleen.

So what now? Recycle something. Take care of yourself and take care of what's around you—even if it's not your job. Remember, we're all in this together...let's make that good news. I will if you will, that's how we start it.

Overlong introductions make *me* crabby.

— NPW

continued from page 1

the tops of their bald heads.
Women who spray their hair into laminated
      helmets.
Drivers who don't use their turn signals.
Drivers who pay more attention to their
      cellular phone arguments than
      to their driving.
Drivers who always use the "HELP! CALL
      POLICE" side of the sunshield.
The tushies for whom Size 3 was invented.
Always finding the toilet seat up.
Being nagged to put the toilet seat down.
Junk mail disguised as government mail.
Junk mail dressed up as urgent telegrams.
Junk mail pretending to be personal mail.

Ed McMahon promising you millions for the
      past ten years and never delivering.
Scratch-off magazine contests that leave
      gold crud under your fingernails.
Waiters who top off your coffee after you've
      gotten the cream and sugar just right.
Campaign promises.
Cockroaches.
Water bugs.
Vampire bats.
Lawyers.

The people who sit down next to you on
airplanes.

The people you wish would sit down next to
you on airplanes.

The very last passenger on the plane taking
the seat next to you.

Starry-eyed romantics who carry large flower
bouquets on trans-continental flights.

The crossword puzzle in your in-flight
magazine already being done.

And wrong. In ink.

Full overhead luggage compartments.

Tray tables that won't go down.

Tray tables that won't stay up.

Commercials on in-flight movies.

The screaming baby behind you.

The captain's garbled announcement.

The instructions for an "ocean landing."

All the scenic views being on the other side
of the plane.

Turbulence during the beverage service.

Beverage carts blocking your dash to the
lavatory.

Turbulence while you're standing in the
lavatory.

Packets of peanuts masquerading as snacks.

Packets of peanuts masquerading as meals.

Ears that won't pop for hours after you
land.

People who don't RSVP.

People who RSVP and then don't show up.

That last ten pounds.

The first ding on your new car.

Glasses that dig into the back of your ears.

Cars nagging "Your door is ajar."

Relatives who drop in.

Relatives who drop in hungry.

Relatives who drop in and won't leave.

Seeing your life in *Cathy* cartoons.

Seeing your life in *Sally Forth* cartoons.

Seeing your life in *The Far Side* cartoons.

Getting clippings from your mother because she sees your life on the funny pages.

Salespeople who hover when you're just looking.

Salespeople who won't take "just looking" for an answer.

Salespeople who can't be found when you know exactly what you want and you're in a hurry.

Salespeople who'll say anything to make the sale.

The "Happiest Place On Earth" costs $27.50 to get in.

Watching the price of movie tickets go up each time you go to the movies.

Huge commercial campaigns to advertise the "true meaning of Christmas."

Leaving a job because of the politics and finding even worse politics in the new job.

Making eye contact with an attractive person across the room, and then seeing that person's date walk up.

Rock concert-goers who throw up on your shoes.

Your hairline.
Your waistline.
Your bottom line.
Your inner thighs.
Car horns that play cute little tunes.
Doorbells that play cute little tunes.
Ice cream trucks within earshot for seven
        tinkly verses.
Painful expensive operations to re-sod your
        scalp.

Bad toupees.
Arrogant tycoons who think fidelity, courtesy
        and income tax are for the "little
        people."
Suspecting you're one of the "little people."
Andrew Dice Clay.
People who pay money to see Andrew Dice
        Clay.
Having something to say and having to say it
        in front of a group.
Having nothing to say and having to say it in
        front of a group.
Half-hour commercials for real estate home-
        study courses.
Mr. Blackwell's Worst-Dressed List.
How "Saturday Night Live" is now compared
        to how it used to be.
The morning after Tequila Sunrises.

It's too late to invent Velcro.

It's too late to invent Liquid Paper.

It's too late to invent The Clapper.

Getting a call from your ex because she wants insight into her current love affair.

Getting a call from your ex because he wants his ring back.

Getting a call from your ex while you're necking with your next.

Bumping into an ex when you look awful.

Finding a mushy card that you didn't send on your lover's night table.

Having to buy feminine hygiene products for friends.

Friends who want to know why you need to stop at the drugstore.

Black roots.

Gray roots.

Having to fold your unmentionables at the laundromat while weirdos watch.

One person in a group needing the joke explained.

Being that one person who needs the explanation.

People who predict the death of your car when you mention the mileage.

People who predict the death of your dog when you mention his age.

Being ill at a friend's house and the only thermometer isn't oral.

Setting off the smoke alarm by opening the oven.

Men who expect women to learn the rules of football but would never learn how to iron a shirt.

Movie reviews giving away the plot.

Movie critics panning everything you loved.

Animal actors making 30 times your salary.
Hearing neighbors fight through
apartment walls.
Hearing neighbors make love through
apartment walls.
Old high school chums who can now buy
you and sell you.
Names that aren't pronounced like they're
spelled.
Names that aren't spelled like they're
pronounced.
People who mispronounce and misspell your
name.
Crusties in your eyes in the morning.
The sound moths make when they land on
the bug zapper.
The sound a wasp makes buzzing inside
your window.
That scary flash when the bulb burns out
just as you flip the light on.
Doctors who keep you waiting.
Trucks too big to see around.
Cars with no brake lights.
Cars with no back-up lights.
Discovering at the wrong moment there's no
honk in your horn.
Yelling an obscenity and realizing your car
window is open.
You're too old to be a famous ballerina.
You're too old to be a famous singing
cowboy.
You'll never slay a dragon.
You'll never be rescued from a dragon by a
knight on a white horse.
People who say, "Let me be honest" and
then aren't.
People who say, "Let me be honest" and
then are.

People who insist on showing their surgical
      scars.
Endless admissions paperwork in the
      hospital emergency room.
Hospital cafeteria food.
Being shaved for surgery.
Prickly new hair growth after surgical
      shaves.
Semi-private rooms that aren't.
Watching your roommate get more "get
      well" cards and flowers than you.
Bedpans.
Cold bedpans.
Tipped bedpans.

Being ignored in nightclubs because your
best friend is cuter.

Anticipating Saturday night's date turning
out to be far better than Saturday
night's date.

Not yet finding the beholder in whose eyes
you are beautiful.

The first day on a new job.

Being "on probation" the first three months
of a new job.

Not getting any vacation days the first six
months of a new job.

Clogged hairspray nozzles.

Christmas merchandise in stores before
Thanksgiving.

Christmas decorations in stores before
Halloween.

Christmas-record commercials on late-night
TV before Columbus Day.

Compact discs costing $15.95.

There are 140 calories in an ounce of
Peanut M&M's.

People on diets who count your calories,
too.

Needing ten hours of aerobics to sweat off
one pound of fat.

Liposuction costing more than you can
afford.

People who never exercise, wearing designer
aerobics outfits to the grocery store.

Tacky personalized license plates.

Undecipherable personalized license plates.

People who laugh through their noses.

People who deliver a punchline just as you
gulp your milk.

Kids spilling their milk.

Kids throwing food in restaurants.

Kids constantly interrupting.

Everyone skinnier than you.
Everyone younger than you.
Everyone smarter than you.
Everyone richer than you.
Everyone better-looking than you.
Tacky movies recycled into feeble TV shows.
Sitcom laugh tracks.
Tattooed eyeliner.
Doctors too busy to answer your questions.
Patients who treat doctors like plumbers.
Anything double-parked.
Redundant office memos that don't even get
        recycled for their paper.
Being pulled out of traffic and ticketed for
        what everybody else is doing.
Cops who smile as they write you tickets.
Healthy sandwiches overstuffed with alfalfa
        sprouts.

Hairy shoulders.
Bristly ears.
Last season's unsold sweaters marked back
        up for this year's unsuspecting buyers.
The first six minutes of car ownership that
        cost you the entire first year's
        depreciation.
Getting hooked on free samples of
        expensive perfume.
Department store perfume squirters.

Movie theater popcorn that smells like old
sneakers.
Bogus butter on movie popcorn.

Stupid dancing popcorn boxes before the
feature movie.
Not being able to read movie credits
because they roll by too fast.
Not being able to read the Roman numerals
on movie credits.
Sticky floors at movie theaters.
Taking 36 shots at an important occasion
with no film in your camera.
Grocery clerks who close out their registers
just as you reach the head of the line.
Men whose socks don't match, who think
they deserve gorgeous dates.
Women who don't keep themselves up, who
think they deserve rich men in high
places.
Term papers.
Midterms.
Finals.
Pop quizzes.
Blue Book tests.
Blue Book tests you didn't study for.
TV news anchors who talk over the credits
of the 9 o'clock movie.

Teenagers who call you "Ma'am."

Teenagers who call you "Sir."

Teenagers who call you "Dude."

Cheerful co-workers first thing in the morning.

Secretaries who would never think to open a dictionary.

Bosses who don't let you get a word in edgewise.

Employees who ask you questions they could easily answer themselves.

An expanding hole in the bottom of your ice cream cone.

Baby talk to pets.

Baby talk between lovers.

Baby talk between lovers in public.

"Winner Notification" scams promising you free exotic prizes if you'll just dial a 900 number costing $4.95 a minute.

"Credit Card Qualification" scams promising you instant credit—even if you're bankrupt—just by calling a 900 number for $39.

Junk faxes claiming big savings on fax paper.

Faxing resumes that anyone can see.

Faxing love notes that everyone can see.

Getting homework faxed to you that parents can see.

Sweat puddles on exercise equipment.

Snarled dental floss.

Shameless public flossers.

Menus listing cutesy names for dressed-up hamburgers.

Menus using flowery adjectives to describe the entrees.

Menus missing the "Today's Special" insert.

Menus not showing prices.

Menus spelling out the prices in words.

Philandering role-model mayors videotaped
taking drugs.

Role-model actors videotaped philandering.

People who refer to themselves in the third
person.

People who refer to themselves as *"Moi."*

People who make change from the collection
plate.

People who don't scoop up after their
pooping pets.

Able-bodied people with fashionable
hairstyles holding "work for food"
signs.

Overpaid sports stars on drugs.

Moles with hair growing out of them.

Magazine ads for nose-hair clippers.

Bogus car phones.

Silly answering machine messages.

Answering machines that cut you off.

Having to punch 36 buttons to make one
long-distance call.

Automated. Phone. Mail. Recordings.

Pay phones that eat your money and don't
work.

Lint, in general.

Other people's belly-button lint, in
particular.

Plaid sport coats.

Instructions printed in four languages, none
English.

Finding out your 1,000-piece jigsaw puzzle is
missing one little piece.

People who light up and then ask, "Mind if I
smoke?"

People who ask, "Mind if I smoke?" and
then light up a cigar.

Smelling like an ashtray after evenings in
nightclubs.

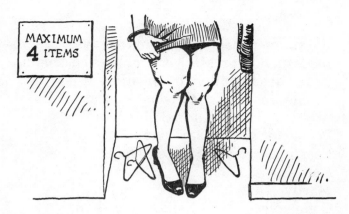

Mini-skirts are back, but your thighs are 20 years older now.

Breaking a mirror.

Finding something on the mark-down rack the week after you bought it retail.

Not being pregnant and people asking when you're due.

Comments like "What a cute little boy" said to your cute little girl.

People who keep plastic covers on their couches and lamp shades.

Bondage lingerie.

Finally completing your classic rock LP collection and everything is now on CD.

Getting CDs as gifts but no CD player.

Taxes on sweepstakes prizes.

Losing a contact lens on a dusty floor.

Recycling papers and finding you need a ton to redeem them for cash.

Middle-aged men with big gold medallions amid forests of gray chest hair spilling out of shirts unbuttoned to the waist.

Middle-aged women dressing like teenagers.

How gray hair looks great on men and old on women.

Those three gray hairs in the front that refuse to pick up the dye.

Hamburger cooked in the microwave.
Bridesmaids' dresses you wouldn't be caught
dead in after the wedding.
People who insist on giving you the details
of their intestinal ailments.
People too good to say "damn."
People married to Prince Charles.
Dan Quayle.
Marilyn Quayle.
Companies that test mascara on bunnies
who aren't even dating.
Activists who ruin ongoing cancer research
by letting bunnies out of cages.
People you've slept with.
People you haven't slept with yet.
People you'll never sleep with.

Handing the keys to your new car to a
suspicious character at the valet lot.
Oil companies that drive up gas prices in
response to every non-related Middle
East political hiccup.
What happens to the right heel of your shoe
driving the car.
Computers that do exactly what you
program them to do.
Computer viruses.
SBD's.
Sounds you can't blame on the dog.

Daddies who won't let the kids play with the model trains.

Mommies who say, "Because I said so."

Kids who keep repeating, "But why? Huh? Why?"

The disappearance of 45 rpm singles.

Vanishing vinyl records.

Used disposable diapers.

Prickly heat rash.

Day-Glo nail polish.

Anything Wedgwood-blue and goose-shaped.

Having to re-take your driver's test.

Loving the wrong people.

Having the wrong people love you.

Jim Henson is gone.

Geraldo's still around.

It's too late to marry Clark Gable or Rick Nelson.

Morgan Fairchild doesn't want you.

Men being not "supposed" to cry.

Secretaries who can't spell.

Delivery men who don't.

Reading the biography of a famous artist and realizing your life is tougher.

Well-paid artists who have their proteges paint and sculpt and sign the artist's names.

Artists who make fortunes scribbling stuff your kid could do.

Women not earning the same paychecks as men for the same work.

Handguns in the wrong hands.

Illegal fireworks at 11 p.m.

Don Rickles is supposedly a really nice guy.

Refrigerator magnets shaped like cows.

Refrigerator magnets shaped like pigs.

People who can eat like pigs and not gain weight.

Men who act like babies when they're sick.
Women who let them.
Mothers who spoil their sons so much it's
    not even worth marrying them.
Men who stay spoiled after age 23 and
    blame it on their mothers.
Parents who obsess over Little League.
Dates who obsess about their exes.
Your blowdryer dying halfway through your
    wet head.
Landlords.
Tenants.
Checks that really are lost in the mail.
Banks charging you $20 because you
    bounced a check 59 cents short.
Banks charging you $4 for depositing
    someone else's bouncing check.
Food warehouses where the price is right,
    but you've got to buy six dozen of
    everything.
Smurfs.
Bad haircuts.
Kids on leashes.
Anti-perspirants that don't.
Musicians who weren't that famous the first
    time, doing comeback tours.
People who poke through the candy
    assortment looking for the filling they
    want.
Callers who address you by the wrong
    gender on the phone.
Friends who throw parties that conflict with
    important football games.
Guests who stay glued to televised football
    games during your parties.
People who pay for top-of-the-line stereos
    and then place the speakers where
    they look nice.

Mary Lou Retton's teeth.

Arnold Schwarzenegger's biceps.

Sylvester Stallone's art collection.

Siskel and Ebert's thumbs.

Roseanne Barr's paycheck.

The sticky brown stuff at the bottom of the refrigerator.

Lukewarm gray coffee with floating white clots.

Houseplants that wait till you take them home to die.

Having to pay for directory assistance.

Having to pay for directory assistance when the operator connects you to the wrong number recording.

Parents who put their toddlers on the phone.

Parents who put their toddlers on the phone when you've called long distance.

THE MAIN MAN

People who wear the hot hairstyle-of-the-month even though it makes them look ridiculous.

Women who breastfeed in public places.

People who get upset about women breastfeeding discreetly in public places.

Women who breastfeed their toddlers till they're five and call it "bonding."

Tossing and turning all night and falling
asleep 20 minutes before the alarm.
Repeated personal questions from people
whose business it isn't.
Postage stamps that won't stick to the
envelope.
Postage stamps that stick to each other.

Gorgeous postcards of locales nowhere near
as appealing in reality.
People who wax nostalgic about their
hometowns but you notice they're not
living there.
People who can only read digital clocks.
"Free gifts" with purchases over $16.
Cab drivers whose sense of direction
magically disappears when you're
from out of town.
Comparisons to photos of you with more
hair and less girth.
People who insist on showing you home
videos of their children's births.
Over and over.
Mothers who never let you forget how much
pain and suffering your birth caused
them.
Men who say they'll call and they don't call.
Women who don't say what they want and
then complain about your choice.

Work that's too hard.

Work that's too easy.

No work.

Women who say money isn't important and
then date only millionaires.

Hearing somebody is making a fortune from
an idea you suggested in a bar.

Algebra.

Physics.

Chemistry.

Trigonometry.

Not remembering anything about the
subjects they made you sweat through
in high school.

Diners who ask their waitresses to make
their food choices for them.

Diners who send back food because the
waitress didn't guess their tastes right.

Madonna's influence on children.

Sandra Bernhard's influence on adults.

Tina Turner looks better after 50 than you
did when you were 20.

Friends who correct your grammar.

Friends who correct your spelling.

Friends who know your grammar and
spelling are faulty and don't tell you.

People who complain about how long their
hair takes to dry because it's so thick.

People who won't show excitement, even
when you tell them great news.

People who don't know how to take a
compliment.

People who don't know how to give a
compliment.

People who love compliments but won't
admit it.

Real sushi never looks as good as the plastic
samples in the window.

Relatives who buy VCRs they can't
program.
Relatives who buy a VCR and want you to
come over and program it for them.
All the good videos are in VHS and your
VCR is a Beta.
Commercials for adult diapers.
Commercials for feminine hygiene products.
Commercials for jock itch powders.
Commercials for diarrhea remedies.
Commercials for denture adhesives.
Commercials with bad actors playing happy
trade school graduates.
Commercials with bad actors playing old
people who fell and can't get up.
Ronald and Nancy getting $2,000,000 plus
free trips to Japan.
Ronald and Nancy getting massive pensions
and Secret Service protection.
Ronald and Nancy.
Doggie breath.
Fishbreath from cats.
Personal idols who turn out to be turkeys in
person.
That time lag between knowing what's
wrong and doing something about it.
Fuzzy pills on sweaters.
The one worn-out place on your otherwise-
good jeans.
Contest mail that gets to you one day before
the deadline.
Contest mail that gets to you one day after
the deadline.
People who live in nicer climates than you.
People who won't apologize.
Not being born rich.
Not marrying rich.
You'll never be rich.

Having to return wedding gifts from people
you hardly know.
Having to buy wedding presents for people
you hardly know.

People who think they're funny.

Bosses who think they're funny.

Prospective in-laws who think they're funny.

People who don't think you're funny.

The millions you coulda made with the Pet
Rock.

Non-English-speaking Customer Service
trainees.

Radio announcers who tell you it's fifteen
minutes past the hour but never say
which hour.

Plastic anti-theft tags deadbolted onto knit
blouses, making it impossible to see
how they fit.

Tags on sunglasses that scratch your face
and obscure your coolness.

$18 shampoos that give you exactly the same
ingredients as the $1.49 stuff.

One-hour photo shops where your snapshots
are displayed in the window as they
come rolling off the machine.

Sales tax.

Property tax.

Income tax.

Surtax.

New taxes disguised as "revenue enhancers."

Too many pennies in your pocket.

Too many pennies in your couch.

Finding out your huge unliftable jar of
pennies is only worth $14.79.

Devil-may-care elevator repairmen.

Oversensitive heat-activated elevator
buttons.

Burnt-out elevator buttons that keep
you guessing.

Stopping at floors with nobody there.

See-thru elevators that leave your stomach
in the lobby.

Gum in your hair.
Gum in your dog's hair.
Dog hair in your gum.
Finding a bug in your bedroom.

Finding a bug in your bed.
Finding a squashed bug in your bed.
Bulging pockets.
People who yawn when you talk.
Practical jokes.
Practical jokes on you.
Not being able to best a practical joker.
Somebody else won this week's lottery.
        Again.
Panhandlers in new Reeboks.
Soggy day-old salad.
Discovering you bought milk with an
        expiration date of yesterday.
Your empty wall space runs up-and-down
        and all your pictures are horizontal.
Not being hungry enough for the "All U Can
        Eat" special.
Eating so much of your favorite food that
        you make yourself sick.
It's cheaper to order the fried-cholesterol
        special than to eat sensibly à la carte.
Sticky fast-food restaurant tables.
Uncomfortable fast-food restaurant chairs.
Fast food.

The way orange juice tastes after you brush your teeth.

Credit cards that are accepted "everywhere" except the place you're in.

Not being able to remember what you had for lunch.

Not being able to remember the song you just heard on the radio.

Friends who watch TV while they talk to you.

It's cheaper to buy new telephones than to repair the old ones.

Birdie souvenirs on your picnic table.

Birdie souvenirs on your car.

Birdie souvenirs on you.

Those hollows around your eyes at night.

That puffiness around your eyes in the morning.

Newspaper ink that rubs off on your hands.

Magazine subscription cards that fall out onto the floor.

Store names with cute spellings of "old."

Store names with cute spellings of "shop."

Overpriced museum gift shops.

You're still 14 to your parents.

You're ancient to your kids.

You're starting to look like your parents.

You're starting to act like your parents.

Men who won't grow up.
Women who think they can change them.
Tight neckties.
Unbroken-in shoes.
Monkey suits.
Streaking windshield wipers.
Pushy sidewalk rose peddlers.
Awful puns you didn't think up first.
Bridesmaids in black.
People who won't leave, but just keep
         talking and walking backwards.
Revenge is considerably less satisfying after
         the first 60 seconds.
No lover will wait as faithfully as your
         sinkful of dirty dishes.
Paying to dye shoes to match dresses you'll
         never wear again.
Personals ad writers who give very broad
         meaning to the term "attractive."
Lies you've told.
Trusting souls who believed you.
Having to remember exactly what you told
         them.
That sinking feeling when you're caught.
Having to show two IDs to cash a check in
         places you've been going for years.
Know-it-alls who don't.
Pushing "Pull" doors.
Pulling "Push" doors.
Tour groups that keep showing up where you
         want to go.
Not being able to smell things when you
         have a cold.
The one double door you try first is always
         the one that's locked.
Record-and-tape clubs that send you order
         forms every three weeks.
For the rest of your life.

Cognoscenti.

Intelligentsia.

Literati.

Glitterati.

PeeWee Herman.

"Ernest" movie marathons.

"KnoWhutImean, Vern?"

"VernVernVernVernVernVernVern."

How come we never see Vern?

People who sit right next to you on empty
buses.

Seat belt buzzers.

Truck backfire.

Flat spares.

Waiters who disappear when it's time for
the check.

Friends who disappear when it's time for the
check.

Tight tippers when the service is good.

Big tippers when the service is bad.

Porters who get a dollar to move your bag
six feet.

Happy-hair newscasters who talk like they're
your buddies.

Weathermen who chit-chat forever before
the forecast.

Special reports that break into your favorite
TV shows.

Special reports that throw off your pre-
programmed VCR taping.

Special reports that have nothing special to
say.

Rex Reed's sneer.

Ed McMahon's laugh.

Sally Jessy Raphael's glasses.

Dud guests on both Phil and Oprah.

Great guests simultaneously on Phil and
Oprah.

Showing up at a party in the same outfit as
someone you hate.
Meeting someone at a party you can't even
make small talk with.
Meeting someone at a party who latches on
to you all evening.
Playing with the dog and later finding out it
had fleas.
Finding out you have spinach in your teeth
after you get home from a party.
Newspaper coupons that don't tear on the
perforations.
Appalachian accents on the flatlands.
Oklahoma accents in Texas.
Texas accents in Oklahoma.
Brooklyn accents anywhere outside
Brooklyn.
Leona Helmsley's 1040.
The Donald.

Corporate CEO's who do their own TV
commercials.
Ed McMahon making zillions from talent
fees, personal appearances and
commercials all year.
Vanna White can buy and sell you
thousands of times.
Your daughter wanting to be like Vanna
White.

Cafeteria janitors mopping while you eat.
Busboys spraying nearby tables with
ammonia while you eat.
Having to yank one napkin out of an
overstuffed dispenser.
Napkin confetti.
Wobbly tables.
Burnt toast.
Soggy toast.
Runny eggs.
Grease-soaked hash browns.
Unshaken orange juice that's mostly water.
Thin maple syrup.
Maple syrup without any maple.
Hard butter tearing your pancakes.
Shriveled, cold and greasy link sausages.
Pancake-and-egg breakfasts served on the
same plate, so the yolk runs onto the
pancakes.
Pancake-and-egg breakfasts served on the
same plate, so the syrup runs onto
the eggs.
High cholesterol.
Curly faxes.
Static electricity shocks.
Overflowing public trash cans.
Walking into a spider's web.
Garbled airport announcements.
Paying 400% markup for wine in
restaurants.
Fancy labels on cheap wines.
Elevator-music versions of your favorite rock
'n' roll rebel songs.
None of the guys in Dockers commercials
have heads.
Getting a run in a new pair of pantyhose.
Suspenders on obese men.
Fishnet T-shirts on obese men.

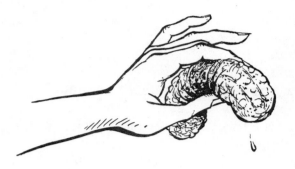

Soggy pickles.
Not-garlicky-enough pickles.
Wonderfully garlicky pickles served to you
        on a first date.
People who eat while they're on the phone.
People who chew gum into the phone.
Commercials on premium cable TV.
Commercials on rented videos.
Commercials on in-school educational TV.
Advertising on restroom stall doors.
Endless fund-raising pledge breaks on public
        TV.
Bicycle messengers.
Jaywalkers when you're driving.
Drivers when you're jaywalking.
Baseball cards your Mom threw away 20
        years ago being worth a fortune now.
Barbie dolls your Mom gave away 20 years
        ago being worth a fortune now.
Tired therapists.
Counselors who dare to have their own
        feelings when yours are the most
        important.
Drifting FM radio reception.
AM radio signals that disappear at the best
        part of the song, just as you enter the
        tunnel.

Yuppies.
Buppies.
Yuffies.
Yuppie wannabe's.
New acronyms for yet another up-and-coming market.
Men who think buying dinner means they're entitled to sex.
Women who think sharing sex means they're entitled to your future income.
Wasps that build nests under your roof near your front door.
Kids who always forget to close the screen door.
Vandalized vending machines.
Vandalized pay phones.
Overpriced concession stands with no competition.
Waiters who try to become your best friend.
Slipped bicycle chains.
Hidden-camera coffee commercials.

T-shirts with stupid drawings.
T-shirts with obscene sayings.
T-shirts with loud advertising.
Liquid non-dairy creamer.
Powdered non-dairy creamer.
The real stuff, that's been on the warm luncheonette counter all day.

Realizing you were short-changed, after you
get home.
The shiny quarter on the sidewalk turns out
to be a bottle cap.
Finding a piece of a ten-dollar bill.
Stepping on chewing gum.
Car ashtrays stuffed with used tissues and
candy wrappers.
Getting stuck in traffic behind a garbage
truck. On a hot day.
The controls in rental cars being in all the
wrong places.
Other people's wedding albums.
Your wedding album, after the divorce.
Dinner parties dominated by one person.
Dinner parties dominated by slide shows.
Dinner parties dominated by screaming
babies.
Pushy wedding photographers.
Amateur wedding photographers.
Clumsy wedding videotape crews.
Your high school graduation picture.
Your driver's license picture.
Candid snapshots with your mouth open and
your eyes half-closed.
People with the same last name as yours
making headlines as criminals.
Clouds of perfume that roll into the room
before and after the wearer.
Pollen.
Hay fever.
Cold sores.
Lawyers.
Jessica Hahn's 900-number confession line.
Endless snaking lines at banks.
Being sick for the office party.
Getting sick at the office party.
Recloseable cereal boxes that don't.

People who slurp soup.

Not being able to slurp soup because other people are there.

Not being able to tip your cereal bowl and zoop out the last of the milk because other people are there.

Packs of teenagers at the mall during school hours.

Packs of teenagers in the convenience store parking lot late at night.

Drive-up restaurant intercoms.

Incomprehensible drive-up restaurant intercoms.

Perfectly clear drive-up restaurant intercoms staffed by non-English-speaking help.

Commercial jingles that run around in your head all day.

Finding out years later that your secret childhood crush had a secret crush on you, too.

Discovering low-fat luncheon meats are high-sodium nightmares.

Places whose biggest attraction is how close they are to better places.

Places supposedly "minutes away," but only at 70 mph with no traffic.

Billboards you pass that proclaim, "If you lived here, you'd be home now."

Doors that stick.

Doors that don't stay shut.

Doors with designer handles you can't grasp.

Carrying your umbrella all day, without it raining.

Plastic upholstery that makes rude noises when you sit.

Everyone thinking the plastic upholstery noise is you.

Losing your glasses, and needing them to find them.

Trying to remember what you just put down, and where you put it.

Trying to remember what you just opened the refrigerator to get.

Having to wait through four lights to make a left turn.

Biting something crunchy in your omelet.

Cleaning the oven.

Having to clean the oven when you move, to get your security deposit back.

Leaving the oven in better shape for the next tenants than it was the entire time you lived there.

Constipation.

Diarrhea.

Rectal itch.

Lawyers.

People who don't return phone calls.

People who do, and you wish they hadn't.

Overdue library books.

Discovering VERY old library books when you're packing to move.

Library book fines.

Getting overdue notices for library books you already returned.

Having to return overdue library books you never even got the chance to open.

Telephone solicitors.

Telephone solicitors calling during dinner.

Telephone solicitors calling during your
passionate moments.

Thin, tasteless milkshakes with all the
calories of thick shakes.

Fast-food chocolate-like shakes made of
space-age acrylic polymers.

People who don't write thank-you notes.

People who don't say thank you.

People who say thank you too much.

Drivers who ask directions and drive away
without saying "Thank you."

Relatives who think writing "Thank you" on
the memo line of a check replaces a
real thank you note.

People who hang up on your answering
machine.

Wanting to leave a message, but there's no
answering machine.

Surprise parties for you.

People who leak surprise parties.

Surprise parties with guests invited from
ancient address books.

Having to thank people you hoped you'd
never see again, for coming to your
surprise party.

Pre-shrunk shirts that aren't.

Pre-shrunk shirts that do, anyway, a little
more each time you wash them.

Shrinks who charge obscene amounts per
hour.

Lawyers who charge obscene amounts per
hour.

Strangers who eavesdrop on your
conversations in restaurants.

Strangers who make comments on your
conversations in restaurants.

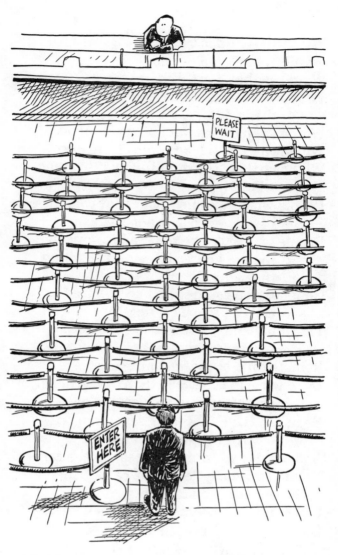

Having to negotiate the velvet ropes at
    banks.
High-fat foods with "LOOK! NO
    CHOLESTEROL!" labels.
Heart-clogging tropical oils in your favorite
    desserts.
Tasteless health food.
Tasteless health food costing more than junk
    food.

47

Windows that don't open.
Windows that don't close.
Windows that don't lock.
Windows that can't be cleaned outside, from
the inside.
Windows that look out onto parking lots.
Windows that look out onto oil refineries.
Windows that look out directly into other
windows.
People who complain about your cooking
but never cook themselves.
People who look like they're listening, but
they're just nodding and grunting in
the right places.
Coupons you could have used before they
expired two days ago.
That tape-and-CD collection you keep
meaning to organize.
Remote control channel jumpers.
Even with 86 channels, there are still only
six things to watch on cable.
Even with the VCR taping, you can only
catch two channels at once.
Ancient dry watermelon seeds in the carpet.
Twisted used staples in the carpet.
Hairballs in the shag carpet.
Paper clips in the vacuum cleaner.
Overstuffed vacuum cleaner bags.
Vacuum cleaner bags bursting all over your
freshly vacuumed carpet.
Learning about a great job from a friend
who's already been picked to fill it.
Sales clerks who talk on the phone while
waiting on you.
Sales clerks who talk to other sales clerks
while waiting on you.
Sales clerks who do you the world's biggest
favor to stop chatting to wait on you.

A letter from the IRS.

A certified letter from the IRS.

A messengered letter from the IRS.

Meeting a delightful attractive single
stranger and discovering he works for
the IRS.

Meeting a delightful attractive single
stranger and discovering she works
for the FBI.

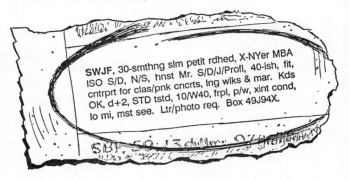

SWJF, 30-smthng slm petit rdhed, X-NYer MBA
ISO S/D, N/S, hnst Mr. S/D/J/Profl, 40-ish, fit,
cntrprt for clas/pnk cncrts, lng wlks & mar. Kds
OK, d+2, STD tstd, 10/W40, frpl, p/w, xint cond,
lo mi, mst see. Ltr/photo req. Box 49J94X.

All those acronyms in personals ads you
can't figure out.

Singles who answer personals ads and lie
about what will immediately become
obvious at first meeting.

Singles who answer personals ads and lie
about what will not become obvious
until much later.

Singles who answer personals ads with
blatant disregard for the truth.

Bringing a disgusting medical problem to a
new doctor who turns out to be cute,
single and your age.

Sleazy nightclubs that stamp patrons' hands
with indelible ink.

Raw spots from trying to scrub off the mark.

Everyone in the office on Monday being
able to see your faded stamp from
the sleazy nightclub.

Sidewalk curbs too high to let you close your
car door.

Having to get out of the car again just to
close the door.

People who fling open car doors without
looking.

Men who don't open car doors for women.

Women who expect their car doors to be
opened for them.

Not knowing whether your date expects you
to open her car door for her.

Not knowing whether you're supposed to sit
and wait for your door to be opened.

No squeegees at self-service gas stations.

Fighting a ticket takes more time and money
than paying the fine and forgetting it.

Having to get used to where everything is in
a new wallet.

Reading an article about the guy you almost
married just making his second
million.

Reading an article about the girlfriend you
dumped becoming Hollywood's
hottest new star.

Your waist being thick and your hair being
thin.

Exes who think they still own you now
because you loved them then.

Upstairs neighbors who vacuum at midnight.

Upstairs neighbors who run their garbage disposal at 1 a.m.

Upstairs neighbors who teach elephants to tap dance at 2 a.m.

Slow leaks.

Flat tires.

Flat spares.

Flat soda.

Flat feet.

Flatulence.

Dust.

Dusting.

Dust bunnies the size of French bread that roll out as soon as guests arrive.

Mail order catalogs full of things you want but can't afford.

Mail order catalogs full of things you want but don't need.

Mail order catalogs full of things you'll never want or need.

Magazines pre-chewed by post office machinery.

Expecting important mail that doesn't arrive.

The check that's still "in the mail."

Only getting mail addressed to "Occupant."

No good news ever coming in an envelope with a window on it.

Magazines selling your name on their mailing lists.

Magazines misspelling your name.

Your misspelled name keeps appearing on tons of new junk mail.

"Please allow 4-6 weeks for delivery."

Having to pay for water at gas stations.

Having to pay for air at gas stations.

The air machine stopping just as you get to the fourth tire.

Mosquitos at outdoor concerts.
Low-flying jets at outdoor concerts.
Lawn seats, after a thunderstorm.
Lawn seats, during a thunderstorm.
Lawn seats, when you're surrounded by
drunken revelers who step on your
hands and spill beer on your date.
Parking meters that don't give you a full
quarter's worth of time.
Parking meters that run too fast.
Meter maids who run too fast.
Meter maids who won't be talked out of
tickets they're about to start writing.
B.O.
Noticing B.O. and realizing it's your own.
Slow drains.
Your hairs in the drain.
Other people's hairs in the drain.
Sardine cans missing their opener keys.
Talking to tellers through bullet-proof glass.
Drivers who could turn right on red and
don't.
Drivers who slow down for green lights.
Slow-reflex drivers ahead of you when the
light turns green.
The only empty parking space for acres and
acres is designated "Handicapped."
Having too many scruples to park in the
handicapped space.
Able-bodied people who have no scruples
taking the handicapped space.
Tired wet used tea bags.
People who flog tired wet used tea bags to
squeeze out that one last cup.
Potato chips you can bend.
Finding green fur on your bread.
Biting into a mealy apple.
Trying to slice a squishy tomato.

How spiked heels feel.
Men who like how spiked heels look
regardless of how they feel.

Escalators, when you're wearing spiked
heels.
Escalators out of service.
Tripping on the uneven risers on out-of-
service escalators.
People on escalators who just stand there
when you want to pass.
Elevators that beep when they pass each
floor.
Talking elevators.
Grocery baggers who put the bread under
the canned ham.
Unpacking an oozing egg carton that was
perfect before it was bagged.
Not finding the TV magazine you bought
the Sunday paper for in the first
place.
Crowds.
Acting wary and suspicious in crowds.
Not acting wary and suspicious in crowds,
and wishing you had.
Having to wait on long lines for things you
want.
Having to wait on long lines for things you
don't want.

Sunroofs that leak.
Milk cartons that leak.
Sugar cones that leak.
Diplomats that leak.

Shaving nicks.
Breaking a nail.
Bending a nail.
Hammering your own nail.
Chipping a nail before you go someplace
        where they'll look at your hands.
Cutting your nails too short.
Hangnails.
Ingrown toenails.
That stuff under your toenails.
That feeling the moment your toe pokes
        through your sock.
That feeling as soon as your pantyhose begin
        to run.
Discovering your favorite sweater has
        become moth lunch.
Service charges on top of all the interest
        that banks make from your money.
Liquid drain openers that don't.
Stripping a stuck screw.
Buying a paper from a coin-box and getting
        yesterday's edition.
Public places not air-conditioned on hot
        humid days.

Missing the bus.
Missing the train.
Missing the plane.
Missing the boat.
Missing the point.
Missing your mommy.
Fantasizing you're somewhere other than
    your dentist's waiting room when he
    calls your name.
The feel of the novocaine shot.
The sound of the dentist's drill.
The sound of that tube sucking your saliva.
"Just X-rays and cleaning" turning into X-
    rays, cleaning and two new fillings.
Bad breath in dentists.
Your dentist waiting till he's up to his wrists
    in your mouth to ask you questions.
Having your mouth packed with cotton
    wadding while your dentist is spouting
    misguided political statements.
Painless dentists who aren't.
Actually paying to have dentists do those
    things to you.
Teeny paper cuts that hurt like anything.
Teeny paper cuts that take forever to heal.
Planes that take off on time when you're
    late.
Plane delays when you're there on time.
"Brief" delays that turn into hours.
Having the airline lose your luggage, and it
    going to a more interesting place
    than you.
Wishing on a star and discovering it's an
    airplane.
Sticky fingers.
Sticky-finger discounts.
Upside-down floating goldfish.
Upside-down floating expensive tropical fish.

People who cough without covering their
mouths.

People who sneeze without covering their
mouths.

People who sneeze, cover their mouths, and
then shake your hand.

Losing your keys.

Losing your wallet.

Losing your passport.

Losing your temper.

Losing a button.

Watching a button pop off and fly across the
room.

Locking yourself out of your car.

Locking yourself out of your house.

Locking yourself out of your house, and
needing to go to the bathroom.

Locking yourself out of your house, and
hearing your phone ringing.

Parking spaces only on the other side of the
street.

Plenty of parking spaces, all off-limits during
rush hour.

Having an old car and a clean driving record
and paying massive insurance
premiums because of your Zip Code.

Hardware superstores with everything but
the one item you need.

Having to stay after school.

Having to go to summer school.

Being left back in school.

False alarms.

False hopes.

False starts.

False friends.

False teeth.

People who take out their false teeth in
public.

Citizens too apathetic to vote.

Citizens who cancel out your vote.

Politicians we're stuck with because they had the best advertising consultants.

Politicians who think we're dumb enough to fall for negative campaign ads.

Politicians we're stuck with because the negative campaign ads worked.

Politicians we're stuck with because we voted for the lesser of two evils.

Congressmen who send you tons of self-serving newsletters.

Realizing your tax dollars pay for all that puffery.

Boring after-dinner speakers.

Boring people who introduce boring after-dinner speakers.

Ballpoint pens that lose their tops.

Felt-tip pens that lose their caps.

People who return your pens with the tops chewed.

Pencil erasers that smear.

Dull scissors.

Loose scissors.

Missing scissors.

Getting the worst haircut of your life right before a special occasion.

Don King's hairdo.

Having to defrost the refrigerator.
Hoary unidentifiable permafrost chunks in
the freezer.
Wrong numbers who call you and get
belligerent because you're not who
they wanted.
Wrong numbers who just hang up when they
hear your voice.
Wrong numbers during dinner.
Wrong numbers in the middle of the night.
Newspaper stories that continue to a page
you don't have.
People who feed pigeons.
People who feed squirrels.
People who use "party" as a verb.
People who "do" lunch.
Biting your tongue.
Coffee so hot your lips burn.
Pizza so hot the roof of your mouth sears.
Salsa so hot your head sweats.
Six-dollar margaritas with 17 cents' worth of
tequila.
Eight-dollar zombies with six-dollar paper
umbrellas.
Paper umbrellas in your eye.
A beer in a bar costing the price of a six-
pack down the block.

Getting your IRS tax forms right after
Christmas.
How the big print giveth and the small print
taketh away.
"...plus taxes and licensing fees."
"...plus shipping and handling."
"...plus dealer prep charges."
"...some restrictions may apply."
"...not available in all stores."
"...sale prices on selected merchandise only."
"...actual mileage may vary."
"Items pictured not actual size."
"Intermediate markdowns may have already
been taken."
"Allow 6-8 weeks for delivery."
"Insurance regulations require..."
"We interrupt this program..."
"Your call will be answered in turn by the
next available agent."
"The number you have reached..."
Screaming, yelling, maniac drag-raceway
commercials.
Yesterday's stale food odors in your
microwave.
Yesterday's cigar odor in your drapes.
Trick candles on your birthday cake.
That writing bump on your middle finger.
Static cling.
Commercials for static cling eliminators.
Uneven sidewalks.
Narrow sidewalks.
No sidewalks.
Sidewalks upended by tree roots.
Deep kisses from smokers.
Hammering in a nail crooked.
Trying to pry out a badly-hammered nail.
Drywall divots.
Furniture dimples.

Getting sand in your bathing suit at the
       beach.
Getting sand in your mouth at the beach.
Getting sand in your tape player at the
       beach.
Derm-abrasion from sand in your sunscreen.
Sand in your bed that night.
Stepping onto 200-degree sand.
Running onto jagged, pebbly sand.
Stepping on sharp, unidentified buried
       objects in the sand.
All dressed up and no place to go.
Movies alone.
Dining alone.
Waking up alone.
Not getting any Valentines after sending out
       a dozen.
Door-to-door candy-selling kids.
Door-to-door cookie-selling scouts.
Door-to-door salvation-selling evangelists.
Someone swiping your welcome mat.
Someone chalking your sidewalk.
Someone smashing your Halloween
       pumpkin.
Someone toilet-papering your mighty oak.
Detours.
Detours with confusing rerouting signs.
Detours that take you through unsavory
       neighborhoods.
Temporary detours that become permanent.
American-made cars with parts from Japan.
Foreign cars manufactured in the U.S.
Trying to figure out which is more patriotic
       to buy.
Breaking a shoelace.
Breaking a glass.
Breaking a leg.
Getting your heart broken.

Near beer.
Flat beer.
Generic beer.
No beer.
Needing to dispose of beer just when she's
     starting to warm to your wit.

Finding out the hard way that the bottlecap
     isn't a twist-off.
Aluminum foil on beer bottle necks.
Bits of aluminum foil in your mouth.
Bottlenecks at toll booths.
Driving into the exact change lane a nickel
     short.
Missing the coin basket.
Setting off the alarm even though you tossed
     in all the coins.
One-way airline tickets costing almost as
     much as the round-trip fare.
Finding out the person sitting next to you
     paid less fare than you.
Forgetting to register your air travel miles
     on the frequent flyer program.
Grotesque flying bugs as big as small planes.
That land on your neck.
Helpful friends who swat insects that land
     on your neck.
Not being able to distinguish between itches
     and insects crawling on your neck.

Tap water not safe to drink.
Tap water that's safe but looks cloudy.
Tap water that's safe but smells funny.
Finding little things swimming in your glass
        of water.
Gypsy moths.
Horseflies.
Yellow jackets.
Lice.
Locusts.
Lawyers.
People who spray when they talk.
Noticing you spray when you talk.
New shoes never feeling as good as they
        look.
Comfortable old shoes too beaten-up to
        wear in public.
Having to choose between unattractive new
        shoes or last year's dated styles.
Shoe salesmen who substitute styles.
Shoe salesmen who substitute sizes.
Shoe salesmen who size your foot with a
        little too much zeal for their jobs.
Too few electrical outlets.
Electrical outlets in hard-to-reach places.
Three-pronged plugs and two-hole outlets.
Octopus wiring rigged at the one convenient
        electrical outlet.
Little speed demons on Big Wheels.
Big speed demons on skateboards.
Your neighbor's cat thinking your flowerbed
        is a litterbox.
People who look around the room when
        you're talking face-to-face.
People who stare at your forehead when
        you're talking face-to-face.
People who stare at your blemishes when
        you're talking face-to-face.

Tangled telephone cords.

Trying to remember where you left the cordless phone.

Cordless phone cross-talk.

Realizing the other conversation is more interesting than yours.

Talking to someone who keeps cutting you off to answer Call Waiting.

Getting your own Call Waiting and having to decide which call to take.

Getting a Call Waiting beep two seconds into a new conversation.

Coming back from Call Waiting only to find yourself in limbo on the other party's Call Waiting.

Getting busy signals calling people who should have Call Waiting.

Poison ivy.

Your hiking companion not getting poison ivy from the same romp in the woods.

Catching poison ivy from burning brush smoke.

Writer's block.

Writer's cramp.

Your doctor's handwritten instructions.

Expensive recipes that take time and effort, and turn out weird.

Having to buy a bathing suit.
Under bright florescent lighting, in front of
        spectators and a triple mirror.
Bathing-suit-shopping depression.

Leaky diving masks.
Bathing suits that slip.
Bathing suits that slip off during dives.
Bathing suits that fill with air bulges
        underwater.
Untimely tumescence in a Speedo.
Butts that shouldn't be in thong swimsuits.
Your butt in a thong swimsuit.
Where thong swimsuits chafe.
That too-light sensation meaning the milk
        carton is nearly empty.
Salad dressing that won't come out of the
        bottle.
Ketchup bottle cap crud.
Ketchup that runs slow but tastes thin.
Ketchup you have to slap out of the bottle.
Slapped ketchup missing the fries and
        landing in someone else's lap.
TV programmers who must think we're
        idiots.
Interchangeable multi-toothed game show
        hosts who must be idiots.
Idiots who win fabulous prizes on quiz
        shows.

The teacher calling on you when you haven't
   done the homework.
The teacher not calling on you when you
   raise your hand.
Somebody else asking the question you were
   going to ask and the teacher saying
   it's brilliant.
People who mispronounce words.
Hearing a word mispronounced and having
   to decide whether to correct the
   person.
Not being sure how to pronounce a word
   and then making the wrong choice.
Smart-alecs who correct you.
Store clerks who say "Have a nice day"
   inflected like "Get outta my face."
Store clerks who say "Let me check" and
   then never return.
Store clerks who say "I'll be right with you"
   and then go on break.
Landlords earning interest off security
   deposits.
Landlords charging for every nail hole, to
   justify keeping the security deposit.
Leaving your address book in a rental car.
Cab drivers who say they have no change.
Repairman who don't show up when they
   say they will.
Taking a day off from work to let in the
   repairmen who don't show up.
People who want your advice.
People who don't want your advice.
People who pester you for advice and then
   don't take it.
Missing that easy lay-up shot into the
   wastebasket.
Overflowing wastebaskets.
Bright track lights over glass-topped tables.

Vending machines with captive-audience marked-up prices.

Vending machines that demand exact change.

Vending machines sold out of what you wanted to buy.

Announcers who blow and tap into the microphone.

Public address systems that squeal loud feedback.

Boomy echoing public address systems that muffle the address.

Blaring ear-splitting public address systems too big for the space.

Concert tickets sold as "partially obstructed view" that turn out to be completely behind the speaker columns.

Concert seats in front of the speaker columns.

Not hearing for two days after you sat in front of the speaker columns.

Hard raisins.

Unseedless grapes.

Chewy peanuts.

Week-old bagels.

Tasteless pizza.

Hard pretzels that are supposed to be soft.

Soft pretzels that are supposed to be hard.

Wedgies.

De-wedging.

People who borrow things but never return
them.

Having to nag people who never return
things.

People who take things without asking first.

Gusts of wind that turn your newspaper
pages before you're done.

Gusts of wind that carry off other sections of
the paper.

Gusts of wind that tip over your half-full
disposable coffee cup.

Bumping into the table and spilling your
drink.

Bumping into the table and spilling everyone
else's drinks.

People who put half-full coffee cups into
wastebaskets.

Finding your girlfriend's number in a public
phone booth.

Finding your boyfriend's number in your
girlfriend's address book.

Finding your own number in a public toilet.

Video games at the entrance to restaurants.

Video games that beckon you with digitized
alien voices.

Video games covered with cigarette ashes.

Video games that eat your quarter.

Video games that cost you 53 quarters just
to figure out.

Shelling out 54 quarters just to earn a free
game.

Vidiots who won't get off the game you
want to play.

Vidiots who flunk in school, but can score
19,489,049,998,589,001 points on
ElectraZork.

People who take forever to tell two-minute
     stories.
People who stop abruptly in front of you on
     the sidewalk.
People who stop abruptly in front of you on
     the road.
Trying to write with a pencil on glossy
     paper.
Wild eyelashes in your eye.
Windblown dust in your eye.
Mascara under your contact lens.
Mascara smudges in raccoon patterns.
People who wear their glasses on strings
     around their necks.
People who wear sunglasses on the tops of
     their heads.
People who wear sweaters tied around their
     waists.
Dudes who wear sunglasses indoors.
Fanny packs that add bizarre bulges to
     silhouettes.
People who leave those tags on pillows and
     mattresses so they don't get arrested.

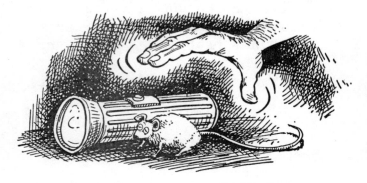

Groping for the emergency flashlight.
Finding your emergency flashlight's batteries
     are dead.
Finding your emergency flashlight after the
     emergency's over.

Itches.

Itches you can't reach to scratch.
Lots of people around, but no one you can
ask to scratch your back.
Itches you can't scratch in public.
An armful of groceries, and an itch on your
nose.
An armful of groceries, and you trip on the
hose.
An armful of groceries, and no one to open
the door.
An armful of groceries, and your keys drop
to the floor.
Bad poetry.
Bed partners who hog the covers.
Bed partners with ice-cube toes.
Bed partners who toss and turn.
Bed partners who snore.
Bed partners who swear they don't snore
because they're asleep while all the
noise is going on.
Bogus holidays created by greedy greeting
card companies.
Mothers-In-Law Day.
Bosses' Day.
Third Cousins' Day.
Getting the cold shoulder for not observing
the latest crass commercial holiday.

Absolutely, immediately, uncompromisingly, non-negotiably, inexorably needing to use a bathroom...

...in traffic, during rush hour.

...during a sermon.

...while in a wetsuit.

...on a job interview.

...at the altar.

Long lines for the ladies' room, none for the men's room.

Having to boldly go where no woman has gone before.

Commercials for lame products masquerading as half-hour cable TV talk shows.

Endless rebroadcasts of commercials for lame products masquerading as cable TV talk shows.

Telephone scams masquerading as cable TV game shows.

Has-beens.

Never-were's.

Never-will-be's.

Has-beens who now have their own cable TV talk shows.

No mute button on your TV remote control.

Droughts.

Water rationing.

People watering their lawns during water rationing.

People washing their cars during water rationing.

Squeezing into a packed subway car.

Finding room to let another person squeeze into the same subway car.

People who don't offer their subway seats to pregnant, elderly or handicapped riders.

Restaurants that refill leading-brand ketchup
bottles with the thin industrial stuff.
Restaurants where a $4.95 order of onion
rings means six on the plate.
Nearly-empty restaurants that seat you next
to the kitchen.
Fully-packed restaurants that seat you
elbow-to-elbow with strangers.
Non-smoking sections at the downwind edge
of the smoking section.
Spouses who only talk and won't listen.
Spouses who don't talk so you can't tell if
they're listening.
Couples who argue loudly at parties.
Couples who smooch loudly at parties.
Couples who end up under coats in
bedrooms at parties.
No parking spaces in the shade.
Having to park your car in the blazing sun.

Touching the steering wheel after your car's
been sitting in the sun.
Frying your thighs on the vinyl upholstery
after your car's been sitting in the
sun.
That first blast from the air conditioner after
you car's been sitting in the sun.
Coming late, after all the well-lit patrolled
parking spaces are taken.

Restaurants that don't have freshly brewed
      decaf.
Getting decaf when you ordered the real
      stuff.

Getting the real stuff when you ordered
      decaf.
Discovering you're out of coffee.
At 7 a.m.
Hard-to-clean coffee stains inside your
      favorite mug.
Car salesmen who smile and won't answer
      questions directly.
Car salesmen who don't know as much
      about the car as you do.
Car salesmen who leave to "check with the
      manager" before killing your deal.
Smiling lawyers who advertise heavily to
      defend drunk drivers.
Smiling lawyers who advertise to help you
      declare bankruptcy.
Smiling lawyers who advertise to help
      motorcyclists sue drivers, "even if it's
      your fault."
Someone else doing your laundry and
      shrinking your favorite shirt.
Someone else doing your laundry and losing
      your favorite shirt.
No one else ever doing your laundry again.

Tailgaters.
Hotdoggers.
Rubberneckers.
Leadfooters.
Brake-riders.
Being stuck behind an RV up a steep
        mountain.
Having an RV on your tail down the other
        side of the mountain.
People who try to one-up your jokes.
People who successfully one-up your jokes.
Victor Kiam's locker-room humor.
The New England Patriots' locker room.
High-paid consultants who make a fortune
        packaging common-sense advice.
High-paid consultants who tell you the same
        things you told your boss last week.
Scruffy strangers approaching your car at
        stoplights brandishing dirty rags.
Scruffy strangers with dirty rags who won't
        take no for an answer.
Feeling obligated to tip scruffy strangers for
        streaking your windshield.
People who wear baseball caps everywhere,
        even indoors.
Dandruff shampoos that don't work.
Dandruff flakes on your dark suit.
Flaky dandruff shampoo commercials.
People who obviously lie about their age.
People who know when you lie about your
        age.
Forgetting where you parked your car.
Forgetting which car you drove that
        morning.
Forgetting to lock your car.
Forgetting to take your keys out of the car
        before you lock it.
Bulky high-visibility steering wheel locks.

Having to do things you dislike because "it would please Grandma."

Having to do things you dislike because it would please your boss.

Having to do things outside your job description for your boss's kid's homework.

Trying to dry yourself with a wet towel.

Putting on clean underwear before you're completely dry.

Wearing a damp bathing suit before you're completely wet.

Having to listen to the entire five-minute multi-screen theater recording because the movie you want is at the end.

Conversation stopping as you walk into the room.

Maps that won't refold along the original creases.

Small-town maps you can only figure out if you live there.

Driving over a state line and suddenly running out of map.

Simplified subway maps designed by abstract artists.

Shopping-mall maps missing the "you are here" arrow.

Why is it so hard for men to find a clitoris?

Having your name misspelled on your diploma.

Exotic locale Hard Rock Cafe T-shirts on people who obviously never went to those places.

Plastic pocket protectors.

The Three Stooges without Curly.

The singing segments in Marx Brothers movies.

Waiters who approach your table with trays
full of other peoples' entrees.
Waiters who choose to have tunnel vision.
Waiters who take the bill and credit card
from the woman and return it to the
man.
Old hippies.
Young yuppies.
Stepping in doggie souvenirs.
Ice cream parlors with dorky names.

Ice cream flavors with dorky names.
Ice-cream-making millionaires who use their
first names so you'll forget they're
franchised conglomerates.
People who bring binoculars to the beach.
That feeling of being watched.
Finding out you are being watched.
Finding out you're being watched by nerds.
Skinny people who talk about how fat they
are.
Fat people who dress as though they think
they're thin.
Politicians who orate to their constituencies
instead of talking to people.
People much younger than you making ten
times your salary.
"Paid commercial programming" that pre-
empts late-night M*A*S*H reruns.

All those spellings of Khaddafy.
All those spellings of Hanukkah.
All those misspellings of your name.
Having a name that everyone makes the
same terrible pun about.
Walking into a wall.
Walking into a wall with lots of people
watching.
All the right people not being attractive.
All the wrong people really revving your
motor.
Randy drunks in singles' bars who hide their
wedding rings.
Getting the "Let's just be friends" rap from
someone you really like.
Great-looking transvestites.
Canceled dates.
Canceled flights.
Canceled credit cards.
Canceled phone service.
Loud sibilant speech.
People who swipe the tip back from the
table.
People whose rear-view mirrors are
obviously aimed for makeup.
Sobriety checkpoints when you're sober and
in a hurry.
People who don't seem to know they're
supposed to change their oil.
People who change their own oil, and dump
it down the public sewers.
Finding out about all your bank's hidden
fees after it's too late.
People who complain about the big-bucks
jobs they fought to get.
Hearing your car making a new noise.
Anyone who pushes your doorbell to witness
for the Lord.

People whose first reaction is "You can't do that."

Parents whose first reaction is "Our house, our rules."

Siblings whose first reaction is "I told you so."

Teachers whose first reaction is "Stay after class."

Spouses whose first reaction is "You're embarrassing me."

Lovers whose first reaction is stony silence.

People who love you but won't say it.

People who love you but won't show it.

People who say "I love you" but don't really mean it.

People who say "I love you" just to get something from you.

Realizing an "I love you" may have a hidden agenda.

Being called "occupant."

Being called "layperson."

Being called "end-user."

Setting off the airport metal detector.

Setting off clothing store anti-theft alarms.

Aggressive urban street vendors.

Aggressive urban panhandlers.

Aggressive urban pigeons.

Pushy Scientologists.

Overcooked fish.
Undercooked chicken.
Having to wait for a drawbridge.
Having to wait at a railroad crossing.
Having to wait for jaywalkers shuffling
across the street.
Having to wait when an oncoming school bus
turns on its flashers.
Athletic supporters that don't anymore.

Little clothes on pets.
Doggie raincoats.
Plaid doggie raincoats.
Wrestling a jumping doggie into his plaid
raincoat.
Putting his raincoat on wrong, and needing
to spot-clean the garment.
Aaron Spelling's contributions to American
culture.
Larry Flynt's contributions to American
literature.
2 Live Crew's contributions to American
poetry.
Black smoke from your tailpipe.
White smoke from under your hood.
Sulfur smoke from the bus in front of you.
Delicious pastry on display, with a fly
buzzing around in the case.

Your little brother tells everyone your real
        age.
Your new bald spot.
Minoxidil working on every head but yours.
Tweezing those stray hairs between your
        brows.
Tweezing those stray hairs at your bikini-
        line.
Speed traps.
Roach traps.
Tourist traps.
No more beer on board, in the middle of the
        lake.
Outboard-motor breakdown, in the middle of
        the lake.
Having to row like a galley slave to get
        ashore from the middle of the lake.
Stupid greeting cards.
Stupid dirty greeting cards.
Schmaltzy greeting cards.
Dumb doggerel poetry greeting cards.
Greeting cards with little paper wheels you
        turn to your age.
The selection of greeting cards left on the
        day before Mother's Day.
Spending your whole lunch hour looking for
        a suitable greeting card.
Mismatched greeting cards and envelopes.
No card costing less than a buck and a
        quarter anymore.
Dribbling gasoline on your shoes at the self-
        service pump.
How your hand smells after pumping gas.
Stepping on something that gives.
Stepping on something that squeals.
Stepping on something that squishes.
When the stairway ends, but you take one
        more step.

Grocery carts with all four wheels going in
different directions.
Grocery shoppers on line in front of you
redeeming six dollars' worth of
coupons.
Grocery shoppers who don't pull out their
checkbooks till the total comes up.
Stubborn grocery scanners that won't read
the price code till the fifth pass.
And then display the wrong price.
Low sneeze-guards at the salad bar.
Cloudy sneeze-guards at the salad bar.
Not being able to identify all the vegetables
in the salad bar.
Your favorite salad bar item is missing.
People who graze as they work their way
through the salad bar.
Gritty spinach.
Spinach salad with leaves the size of
elephant ears.
Holes in your pocket.
Holes in your muffler.
Holes in your argument.
Squeaky beds.
Your next-door neighbors' squeaky beds.
Getting a brilliant idea in your sleep and not
remembering it in the morning.
Getting a brilliant idea in your sleep that
makes no sense in the morning.
Waking in the middle of a tantalizing dream
and not being able to bring it back.
Trying to cut out a newspaper article
continued on the back of the same
page.
Motel room paintings.
Motel rooms with Bibles but no phone books.
Mildew.
Mildew you can smell but can't find.

Dropping the soap in the shower.
Having to share a towel.
Being the second to share the towel.
Loud bathroom exhaust fans that
        automatically go on with the light.
Bathroom exhaust fans that don't work
        when you need them to.

Bone-crushing handshakes.
Wet-fish handshakes.
Extending a handshake and the other
        person ignoring it.
Being introduced by the wrong name.
Being introduced by a nickname you don't
        like.
Being introduced by a childhood nickname
        you wish everyone would forget.
Forgetting a friend's name in mid-
        introduction.
Fastfood drive-up windows that don't pack
        plasticware for your meal.
Fastfood drive-up windows that don't pack
        ketchup for your fries.
Carry-out soup containers that leak.
Staples that won't pierce a sheaf of papers.
Breaking nails removing staples.
Holes in your shoes.
Pebbles in your shoes.
Snow in your shoes.

Red-eyed snapshots.
Blurry vacation photos.
Photos fogged by airport X-ray machines.
Thumbprints on your reading glasses.
Large, gaudy pinky rings.
Sharp-edged pinky rings.
Tough-to-inflate balloons.
Balloons that pop before they're full.
Trying to ripen not-quite-ripe fruit at home.
Fruit that goes from green to rotten without
        passing through ripe.
Tourists clogging up your sidewalks.
People treating you like a tourist when
        you're visiting.
People calling themselves "natives" after
        living someplace three years.

Cutesy restroom signs that leave you
        wondering which door is for you.
Grown women who use cutesy terms for the
        bathroom.
Grown women who use cutesy terms for
        going to the bathroom.
Grown men who say they have to go to the
        little boy's room.
What foreigners must think of grown men
        heading to a room for little boys.
People who stand right behind you waiting
        for the urinal.

82

Restaurants that turn up the air conditioning
to make you leave.

Restaurants that begin putting chairs on
tables while you're still eating.

Bars that turn up the lights to make you
leave before you've finished your
drink.

Tossed salad that's all lettuce.

Lo-cal dressings that taste like it.

Dollar-a-draft beer served in 8-ounce
glasses.

Wax museums.

Tourist buses that stop at wax museums.

Gas station restrooms.

Having to ask for the key to a gas station
restroom.

People you don't want to see who keep
popping into your life.

People who read over your shoulder.

People who shift positions so you can't read
over their shoulders.

Friends who borrow money and never repay
you.

Worrying whether it's petty to ask them to
repay you.

Needing friends to repay large sums of
money they've apparently forgotten.

Food exploding in the microwave.

Hot pan handles.

Melting pan handles.

People who defend their stupidity with
arrogance.

Itchy wool sweaters.

Shirts that allow the itches to get through.

Cashiers who can't calculate change without
help from the register.

Thinking it's Friday morning when it's only
Wednesday.

The phone ringing just as you put the key in
the lock.
The answering machine clicking on just as
you pick up the phone.
The doorbell ringing just as you get into the
tub.

Bicyclists wearing Walkmans.
Drivers wearing Walkmans.
Drivers glued to Watchmans.
Tape-eating car stereos.
Tape-eating VCRs.
The cost of new tapes.
Weighing exactly the same after a solid week
of dieting.
Getting drenched at the curb by a car hitting
a slushpuddle.
Dropping an egg.
Stubbing your toe.
Hitting your funnybone.
Skunk stink in the wind.
Post-it notes that have lost their stick.
Unscrewing a hot lightbulb.
Housemates who never close cabinet doors.
Roommates who never close dresser
drawers.
Guys who never hang up wet towels.
Women who hang pantyhose over the
shower curtain rod.

Bogus clergy pushing contribution buckets
in your face at the airport.
Shaven misguided cult followers in saffron
robes slam-dancing ecstatically in
airports, handing you flowers and
then asking for donations.
Well-dressed airport petition-pushers
promoting nuclear power and Jane
Fonda's destruction.
Jane Fonda's thighs.
Ted Turner's mouth.
Fading football heroes telling Supreme
Court justices to "loosen up."
Fading football oddsmakers turning into
eugenics professors.
Fantasies that take too much money to
make real.
Fantasies that take too much effort to make
real.
Fantasies that take too much courage to
make real.
The Sixties clothing you finally threw out is
back in fashion.
Missing the weekly garbage pickup.
Missing the last mail pickup.
Cake-like brownies.
Overpriced designer brownies.
No more brownies.
Stains that won't come out.
Your horoscope promising excitement and
romance.
Your ex's horoscope promising money and
happiness.
People who order two drinks and the most
expensive entrees and then want to
split the check equally.
People who thank the Lord for favors you
did for them.

Co-workers who say, "But that's the way we always did it."

Managers who say, "We tried that once and it didn't work."

Associates who say, "It sounds good to me, but the boss will never go for it."

Bosses who say, "Let's run it past the lawyers."

People who keep making the same mistakes.

Being one of those people.

Rollercoaster hormone swings.

Being with someone on that rollercoaster.

Selfish sex partners.

Clumsy sex partners.

Unwashed sex partners.

No sex partners.

The people who used to live in your new home getting more interesting mail than you.

People who can eat all they want and never gain an ounce.

People who can eat anything they want and never break out.

People who can eat whatever they want and live to be a hundred.

Shortcut ways to spell "light."

Shortcut ways to spell "easy."

Shortcut ways to spell "through."

The more money you make, the more money you need.

The interest on your credit card balances.

Bizarre gifts from your boyfriend's mother.

Trying to figure out what gift to buy your boyfriend's mother.

If you don't want to iron, you have to wear polyester.

Opening a box of crackers and finding more broken than whole.

Missing street signs.

Non-visible house numbers.

One-way signs that point the wrong way.

People who give directions saying "turn east" instead of "turn right."

Signs that say, "Back in 15 minutes."

Waiting 15 minutes and no one coming back.

Kids who whine, "Are we there yet??"

Kids who get there and whine, "I wanna go home!!"

Kids who always bug you to buy them things.

Kids who are perfectly quiet till you get on the phone.

Kids who always ask for water before going to bed.

Kids who always wet the bed.

Blind dates with "good personalities."

People who think they're "way cool."

Co-workers who play video games at work.

Secretaries who watch TV at work.

Having nothing to do at work and no TV to watch.

Television exit polls.

Left-over election posters.

Left-over election bumper stickers that don't peel off.

You shoulda worn braces.
You shoulda paid better attention in math
    class.
You shoulda lost that weight when you were
    younger and it was easier.
You shoulda started that IRA years ago.
You shoulda listened to your dad.
You shoulda taken Door Number Three.
Icky gel on canned ham.
Trying to get the ham out of the can.
Tinned-meat cans with tiny keys and sharp
    edges.
Meat can keys that break off half-way
    around.
Impossible-to-turn can openers.
Dirty can lids that dunk down into the soup.
Obscene phone callers with no imagination.
Letter writers who dot their i's with little
    circles, hearts or smiley faces.
Letter writers who end every sentence with
    exclamation points.
Postcards with very personal messages.
People don't write letters any more.
Plastic forks that can't take the pressure.
Paper plates that can't take the forks.
People who store chewing gum behind their
    ears.
Visible panty lines.
Shifty baby sitters.
Drunk, off-key singers who won't hand over
    the Karaoke microphone.
Seeing Richard Simmons on every spin
    around the TV dial.
Seeing that real estate guy in the toupee on
    every spin around the TV dial.
Seeing Gilligan in another easily avoidable
    stupid situation on every spin around
    the TV dial.

Feeble old security guards.
Cocky young security guards.
Power-hungry security guards.
Sirens going down your street.
Sirens stopping on your street.
Police helicopters hovering overhead.

Suction-cup Garfields grinning at you from
the car in front of you.

Charlie Manson look-alikes grinning at you
from the car behind you.

Christy Brinkley look-alikes ignoring you
from the car to the left of you.

Over-eager waiters who reach for your plate
before you've finished.

The question-and-answer portion of the Miss
America Pageant.

Opening soda cans you didn't know had been
shaken.

Open soda cans that attract brazen yellow
jackets.

Fruitcakes as Christmas presents.

Fruitcakes as dates.

Fruitcakes as bosses.

Bosses who still expect you to fetch coffee for
them.

Seeing your ex on Lifestyles of the Rich &
Famous after you filed for divorce in a
no-alimony state.

Sloppy drunks at parties.

People who arrive at parties already drunk.

Married drunks who try to pick you up.

Novice drunks who can't hold it.

Sentimental drunks who cry.

Dangerous drunks who think they can drive.

Dried-out bran muffins.

Thinly-filled sandwich cookies.

Chipless chocolate chip cookies.

Microwaved Thanksgiving turkeys.

Ruler scars from parochial school.

The latest trendy diet.

Self-enrichment seminar junkies.

Self-enrichment cassette tape junkies.

People who buy into every self-enrichment
program and never get enriched.

Warm soda.
Cold chianti.
Atonal music.
Eddie Murphy's laugh.
Sneaky tacked-on service charges on concert
tickets.
Seeing people at concerts who obviously
came only because of free tickets, and
you paid a fortune for yours.
People standing on seats in front of you.
The drunken stoned seat-holders next to you
borrowing your expensive binoculars.
The singing of people behind you drowning
out the group you came to hear.
200-pound women in horizontal stripes.
200-pound women in vertical stripes.
400-pound men who don't wear shirts.
The fact that looks shouldn't matter, but
they do.
Being the only hotel guest not with the Miss
Monster-Truck-Parts Regional
Pageant.
People who borrow your coffee mug and
return it with brown stains.

Coffee mugs with cute sayings.
Being expected to make the office coffee.
Finding an empty pot sizzling on the
coffeemaker burner.

Ted Koppel's hair.
Prince Charles's ears.
Karl Malden's nose.
Morton Downey Jr.'s teeth.
David Letterman's gap.
The garage mechanic switching your car
        radio to a rap music station.
The parking valet adjusting your seat to his
        legs.
Forgetting to pack your sunglasses.
Forgetting to pack your contact lens case.
Forgetting to pack your birth control.
People who take board games too seriously.
People who take golf too seriously.
People who take themselves too seriously.
Your girlfriend's parents starting to give you
        those in-law eyes.
Dinner guests who announce they're on diets
        just as you begin to serve your seven-
        course feast.
Trying to find a good deli in Texas.
People who think they know good pizza.
Fake bacon bits.
Imitation crab legs.
Artificial cheese.
Ballpark nachos.
MSG headaches.
Born-again anythings.

Guests who sit in your favorite chair.
Guests who straighten your pictures.
Guests who put their feet up on your
    furniture.
Relatives who rearrange your furniture.
Nasty grandparents.
Cheap grandparents.
Bickering grandparents.
Moms who can't cook.
Dads who can't cook.
Teens who won't cook.
Tourists with funny accents who claim you
    talk funny.
People who pronounce "R's" in words without
    them.
People who leave "R's" out of words with
    them.
People who argue that gas grills are better
    than charcoal barbecues.
People who want to ban books they haven't
    read.
Five-day weather forecasts that are never
    accurate.
Nail polish chips, two hours after your
    manicure.
White packing peanuts, all over your floor.
Styrofoam cups will outlive your
    grandchildren.
Not enough people recycle.
There aren't enough places to recycle.
Pay-before-you-pump self-service gas
    stations.
Full-service gas station attendants who have
    to be asked for full service.
Living just outside the free-delivery zone of
    your favorite take-out place.
Microscopic organisms living inside your
    socks.

Your gums are receding.

Your hairline is receding.

Your coastline is receding.

Angie Dickenson doesn't seem to age.

Dick Clark doesn't seem to age.

You are aging rapidly.

There is no painless way to remove hair from your legs.

Needing "C" batteries and having only "D" cells.

The stupidest person in the office getting promoted.

Construction workers thinking their wolf whistles are compliments.

Movie stars using their celebrity to promote political views.

Movie audiences cheering at scenes of gruesome stabbings but squirming at shots of medical injections.

The garbage disposal chewing another spoon.

The dog destroying another pillow.

The city tearing down another landmark.

Stoplights on expressway entrance ramps.

People who only talk about their therapists.

People who only talk about themselves.

People who only talk about what they watch on TV.

People who say "umm" after every third word.

People who lie by omission.

Getting hit by air conditioner drips.

Not getting good TV reception unless you cough up for cable.

Coughing up even more for pay-per-view.

Flight attendants with attitudes.

Bus drivers with attitudes.

DMV clerks with attitudes.

Movies supposedly set in New England, showing cars with California plates.
Movies supposedly set in your hometown, with no recognizable landmarks.
TV camera shots with microphone shadows.
Turning off the ignition with the power windows still open.
Turning off the ignition but the engine keeps running.
Keys that break off in locks.
Trying to find the right key on a ringful.
Mistaking the trunk key for the door key. In the rain.
Not noticing you've stepped in something till you're in the car.
Getting a chain letter.
Breaking a chain letter.
Having to make your own coffee in the morning.

Having to wait while the coffee brews.
Trying to separate coffee filters.
Spilling ground coffee.
Spilling wet coffee grounds.
Empty "Give-a-penny, take-a-penny" cups at cash registers.
Mail-order fashions that come looking nothing like their catalog pictures.
Getting something caught in your zipper.

Get-rich-quick pyramid schemes that pay
everybody before you.
Pyramids that get busted just as your level
is about to hit paydirt.
Rushing to a mailbox that turns out not to
pick up till the next day.
Postage rates going up again.
Postage rates going up right after you buy
three rolls of stamps.

This stamp, plus 29¢ postage, 4 box tops, your receipt (with your purchase price circled) and a note from your Mom, is equivalent to the 'G' stamp rate.

Ugly temporary postage stamps.
The ugly taste of postage stamps.
Stamps featuring famous people you've
never heard of.
You can't take your postal business to
another company.
Drive-in movie speakers that conk out
halfway through the film.
People who demand you define your terms.
Incessant whining on thirtysomething.
Polyester pills.
Polyester-pill shavers.
Your mother telling you to wear a sweater
because she's cold.
And she always will, for the next 40 years.
Hearing yourself say what your Mother
would have said.
Hearing yourself say what your Father
would have said.

Car breakdowns in seedy neighborhoods.
Emergency road service taking three hours
to respond to your call.
And telling you to wait in your car.
Hitting another car right after dropping
your collision coverage.
Millions of America's youth seeing Bart
Simpson as a role model.
Movies edited for TV, to inhibit the sex.
Movies edited for TV, to kill the violence.
Movies edited for TV, to pack in more
commercials.
Computer dating junk mail after you're
married.
Computer-generated junk mail to your
spouse, but you're not married.
Scientology personality tests.
Alternative-company pay phones that charge
more for less service.
"Happy Birthday" sung loudly by waiters
who don't know your name.
Finding a greeting card perfect for a friend
but inscribed, "Happy Birthday,
Gramps."
Finding greeting cards for every occasion
except the one you're looking for.
Shopping mall survey takers.
Diesel engines belching soot.
Mothers and daughters who dress alike.
Losing 10 mpg because of your car's power
accessories.
Overly permissive parents who let their kids
run amok in their homes.
Overly permissive parents who let their kids
run amok in your home.
Parents who walk on eggshells for their kids.
Parents who walk on hot coals for their kids.
Kids who walk all over their parents.

Overtime hours with no overtime pay.
The last eight weeks of pregnancy.
Ant traffic on your kitchen counter.
Ant clusters on your kitchen floor.
Antless ant traps.
Telethons that pre-empt The Three Stooges.
People who discourage you, claiming to have
your best interests at heart.
People who only call you when they want
something.
Lumpy gravy.
Lumpy rice.
Lumpy Rutherford.
Hitting the wrong button on the food
processor and pulverizing what you
meant to chop.
Hitting the wrong button on the word
processor and vaporizing what you
meant to save.
The video you want to rent being out again.
Spandex pants on inappropriate fannies.
Pot-bellied men in Speedos.
Designer jeans on four-year-olds.
Non-profit organizations that send you
solicitation letters every six weeks.
Donating to a non-profit organization, and
getting new solicitation letters every
three weeks.
Turning down a couple's invitation because
you love her, hate him.
Accepting a couple's invitation because you
love her, hate him.
Light spring fashions on display in stores in
dead of winter.
Heavy wool suits on display in stores in
sweltering summer heat.
Bathing suits being all sold out at the height
of bathing suit season.

Taking your little nephew to the zoo and finding the larger animals are mating that day.

Women who throw parties for plastic dishes
that burp.

Best friends who sell Mary Kay cosmetics, so
you have to buy $78 worth of goo.

Makeup not doing anything for you that it
did for the magazine model.

"Waterproof" mascara that leaves the tracks
of your tears.

Blinking before your mascara dries, so you
get those little black dots underneath
your eyes.

Gummy bears.

Gummy worms.

Gummy anything caught in your back teeth.

Seeing people use toothpicks.

Seeing people use forks as toothpicks.

Seeing people use toothpicks as fingernail
cleaners.

Seeing people clip their nails.

Hearing people clip their nails.

Finding nail clippings all over your
bathroom.

Running out of gas.

Running out of money.

Running into an old friend who asks you for
money.

Trying to write legibly in a car.

Not being able to read your own
handwriting.

Sealing the envelope with the bill inside
backwards, so no address shows
through the window.

Presents that break before you get the
thank-you notes written.

Presents that get eaten before you get the
thank-you notes written.

Presents that die before you get the thank-
you notes written.

Joan Collins may someday age like a normal woman.

Mel Gibson will eventually age like a normal guy.

Christopher Reeve will eventually age like a mortal man.

American-born citizens who don't know the words to the national anthem.

Naturalized citizens who know more about civics than you.

Really being sick the day after you took a sick day off work.

Blemishes that announce your cycles or binges to the world.

Recopying dozens of names and numbers into your new address book.

White hose on anyone but nurses and children.

When you pull that little thread and a button comes off.

When you pull that little thread and your sweater gets a hole in it.

Obscure acronyms.

People who speak in jargon at cocktail parties.

Popcorn in your teeth.

Cowlicks.

Dingleberries.

The dog yanking you for the entire walk.
The dog wanting the longest, most vigorous
walks on the nights you're most
exhausted.

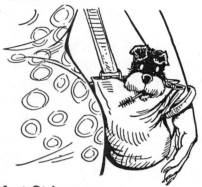

Dogs that fit in purses.
Dogs named Fifi and Muffy.
Smokers with attitudes.
Non-smokers with attitudes.
Ex-smokers with a mission.
Quitting smoking and instantly gaining ten
pounds.
Liquid-drink diets that let you eat "one
sensible meal a day."
"One sensible meal" being all the rabbit food
you can eat.
Sensible shoes.
Nerdy, know-it-all proofreadrs.
Meeting a knowledgeable, helpful insurance
agent who can save you money and
you've already signed on with a yutz.
Discovering the optional insurance charge
makes your $19.95/day car into a
$32/day rental.
Not knowing whether your personal
insurance policy makes that charge
unnecessary.
Six-year-olds who can open child-proof caps
that you can't.

Thunderstorms booming over your house.
What the dog does under the bed during
thunderstorms.
Lightning power-surges into your television.
Exes without the courtesy to drop dead or
move to another planet.
Brand new cars that hog two spaces in
parking lots.
Little red dents on your nose from your
glasses.
Non-English-speaking bank tellers.
Cold sufferers next to you on the bus.
Condoms.
No condoms.
Finding out $50 too late that one rose
delivered to the office has as much
impact as a dozen brought home.
People who doodle in library books.
Pages missing from library books.
The used textbooks you bought for the
highlighting are underlined at all the
wrong points.
Not being able to remember all the words to
"Strawberry Fields Forever."
Realizing you never knew all the words.
Indigestion and heartburn.
Commercials for antacids that give you
indigestion.
Discovering the inside of an Oreo cookie is
lard and sugar.
The way Hollywood treats talented actresses
over 40.
Women having to choose between Career
Track and Mommy Track.
Men not having to choose between career
and family.
Guests who bring screw-top wines to your
dinner parties.

Interior decorators named Bunny.
Landscape architects named Rod.
Waterbed salesmen named Slick.
News anchors named Muffy.
Anyone named Bitsy.
Or Trip.
Or Trey.
People who assume you want to be called by
a nickname.
People who take it on themselves to invent
nicknames for you.
Bra straps slipping off your shoulder.
Slips that fall two inches below your
hemline.
Half-slips that ride up around your waist.
Pantyhose designed with the crotch at the
knees.
Pantyhose with four inches of wrinkly ankle
slack.

Tangled wire clothes hangers.
Pins on the dressing room floor.
Other people's try-ons piled on the dressing
room floor.
No dressing-room hooks for hanging up your
clothes.
Saleswomen who follow you into the lingerie
fitting room.
Only one mirror for six dressing rooms.

Sure-seal storage bags that don't.
Self-stick labels that won't.
Self-starting charcoal that doesn't.
Fool-proof recipes that aren't.
Dripless spouts that are.
Fuel-efficient cars that aren't.
Creamy blue eye shadow.
Sparkly green eye shadow.
Heavy black eye shadow.
Make-up artistes who draw in cheekbones.
Make-up amateurs who can't draw lipstick
        inside the lines.
Totally moronic hints from hometown paper
        Heloise-wannabe's.
Totally useless advice from local-paper Dear
        Abby clones.
Totally unfunny stories from regional Dave
        Barry copy-cats.
"No fat chicks" bumper stickers.
"If you're rich, I'm single" bumper stickers.
"I brake for hallucinations" bumper stickers.
"As a matter of fact, I DO own the sidewalk"
        bumper stickers.
The volume always being louder on the TV
        shop-at-home channel.
Holier-than-thou Bible-thumpers blocking
        your way into the malls.
Canned mushrooms.
Unsalted anything.
People who carry beepers but don't have
        vital jobs.
People who let their beepers beep more than
        three times, just to let everyone know
        they're important.
Morning DJs who think they're funny when
        they're just dumb and dirty.
Plastic wrap all wrapped up to itself.
Plastic people all wrapped up in themselves.

Nail polish bubbles.

Time-share come-ons.

Non-English-speaking gas station attendants.

Non-English-speaking gas station attendants
trying to give you directions.

Latch-key kids hanging out at malls.

Nintendo addicts.

Five o'clock shadow on your legs.

Adhesive bandages that take your body hair
with them.

Waking up at 6:30 a.m. on Saturdays.

Movies that sell out after you've waited an
hour on line.

The fourth corner of the fitted sheet that
doesn't fit.

How your hair looks absolutely great the
day you make an appointment to get
it cut.

Intestinal gas on a first date.

First dates with intestinal gas.

Whisperers with bad breath.

Not being able to tell people they have bad
breath.

Finding a bottle of mouthwash someone has
planted on your desk.

People who press on your bruise and say,
"Does that hurt?"

Pimples that manage to show up for special
occasions.

Craving a kind of candy bar that's not made
anymore.

Nickel candy bars costing 60 cents now.

Clothes that shrink.

Clothes that stretch.

Rainstorms right after you wash your car.

Underdressing for religious services.

Overdressing for bowling.

The color scheme for bowling shoes.

The neighbor's kids wanting to sell you
     candy.
The neighbor's kids wanting to swim in your
     pool.
The neighbor's kids wanting 25 bucks to cut
     your lawn.

Your cat bringing you small dead animals as
     presents.
Co-workers who borrow change for the
     vending machine. Every day.
Commercials at the front of rented videos.
Forgetting to return rented videos.
Forgetting to return rented videos you
     haven't watched.
People with no sense of direction.
People with no sense of humor.
People with no sense.
Bicyclists who edge joggers off the paths.
Cars driving in the bicycle lane.
You're too old to compete in the Olympics.
The lifeguards not ogling you anymore.
They're all too young for you now, anyhow.
Freezer burn.
Windburn.
Heartburn.
Rope burns.
Rug burns.
Slow burns.

Foreign films with dubbed voices that don't
match the mouth movements.
Foreign films with dubbed voices that don't
match the characters' looks.

I would like to go out with you.

Foreign films with translations that couldn't
possibly be the dialogue the
characters are saying.
Highly-acclaimed foreign films that make no
sense.
Party invitations that say BYO.
The keg running dry a quarter of the way
into the party.
The hostess asking you to bring tapes to the
party and no one wanting to hear
them.
Men who say, "Better close the barn door
before the horse gets out."
People who say, "It's snowing down south."
Women who say, "My friend is visiting."
Socks that stop two inches below your pants
when you cross your legs.
Unreachable burned-out refrigerator light
bulbs.
Light bulbs supposed to last 750 hours, but
there's no way to check.
Ubiquitous oat bran health claims.
Everything tasty being bad for you.
Everything flavorless being good for you.

Boxer shorts that slip down around your
hips.
Low-rise briefs that fit you funny below the
waist.
Micro-briefs that you don't quite fill out.
Rest stops too far apart on long car trips.
Dog souvenirs on the jogging trail.
Horse souvenirs on the bicycle trail.
Cow souvenirs on the nature trail.
Fruit-scented styling mousse.
Pine-scented bathroom spray.
Ammonia-scented perming lotions.
Frozen fish being sold as "fresh."
Crabcakes that are 1% crab and 99% cake.
Mouthfuls of tiny bones in fish fillets.
Mouthfuls of tiny bones in fish fillets on first
dates.
Harmonic Convergence hoopla.
The possibility of a second Harmonic
Convergence.
Power breakfasts.
Power trips.
Power plays.
Friends who bug you till you advise them.
Friends who offer more advice than you
asked for.
Friends who ask for advice and then blame
you if it doesn't work out.
Friends who don't follow their own advice.
Parents who give their kids strange names,
and there's not even a rich relative
involved.
Parents who name their kids after consumer
products.
Candy that turns your tongue blue.
Designer jellybeans costing $6 a pound.
Neon-colored designer jelly beans that taste
like perfume.

People who ask you if you're feeling well
when you thought you looked great.
People who peer into your face and say you
look tired.
Having to say something back to people who
say you look tired.
People who label your personal traumas
"just a phase."
People who tell you things "for your own
good."
Parents who say, "This will hurt me more
than it hurts you."
Artificial coloring.
Artificial flavoring.
Artificial people.
Never seeing any more money from the
Tooth Fairy.
Being on the receiving end of guilt trips.
Feeling guilty for laying guilt trips on
someone.
Never having occasion to use the good china.
Streets that come to abrupt ends, but pick
up again two blocks later.
Streets that suddenly change names.
Getting lost because nobody told you the
street changes names.
Looking for an address and the house
numbers suddenly jump ahead
several hundred.
Getting directions to expressways using
their names, and the signs only
showing numbers.
The chiropractor wanting you back for 60
more visits.
Doctors being unable to do a thing for your
virus except letting it run its course.
And you still have to pay for the office visit.

Drivers who flash their brights in your
    rearview mirror.
Oncoming drivers who won't dim their
    brights.
Your own brights being on for miles.
Drivers who turn on their fog lights when
    there's no fog.
People who pronounce the "L" in salmon.
People who pronounce both "R's" in
    February.
Paying to see pop stars who lip-synch.
Not being able to figure out where that foul
    smell is coming from.
Pick-up lines.
Tired pick-up lines.
Pick-up lines you heard in high school, being
    said 20 years later by grown men.
Being unable to think of better pick-up lines
    than the ones you used in high school.

People who call you and put you on hold.
Having to listen to sappy elevator music on
    "hold."
Enjoying a good tune on "hold," and getting
    interrupted by a voice.
Being around eternal pessimists.
Being around eternal optimists.
Being around the terminally apathetic.

The guy on the bar stool next to you having
a bad attitude.
Oily orange cheese-puff dust that won't come
off your hands.
More chips than dip.
More dip than chips.
Biting down hard on an olive you mistook for
pitted.

You're stuck with your relatives.
Realizing you're doing all the work in a
	"group" project.
Company picnics.
Company games at company picnics.
Pelvic exams.
Hernia checks.
Stomach cramps.
Charleyhorses.
Jock itch.
Politicians.
Mediocre motivational seminars.
The quality of food at most dinner theaters.
The quality of theater at most dinner
	theaters.
Dates who kiss like fish.
Dates who kiss like vacuum cleaners.
Dates who kiss like irrigation projects.
None of your neighbors paying attention
	when your burglar alarm goes off.
All of your neighbors getting angry at you
	when your car alarm goes off.
The smell of hair-removal potions.
Susan B. Anthony dollars.
Honor-bar bills.
Two-dollar bills.
Two-day stubble.
Two-day-stubble burn.
Five-o'clock shadow at two o'clock.
Hair gaps that keep you from ever growing a
	full beard.
Rap music that goes platinum from
	censorship hype instead of quality.
Conditional agreements.
People who make conditional agreements
	and then unilaterally change the
	conditions.
People who smell like their lunch.

Yet another Barbara Walters special.
Yet another magazine article on "The New
Woman."
Yet another article speculating on Cher's
plastic surgeries.
Yet another article about Elvis sightings.
Yet another article about two-headed
Siamese alien-seed test-tube UFO
genius babies.
Having to ask for what you want.
Having to ask for what you want, and
nobody listening.
Actually getting what you want, when you
don't want it anymore.
All the wrong men in muscle shirts.
All the wrong men in bow ties.
All the wrong men in Corvettes.
All the wrong men calling for dates.
Losing your "to do" list.
Not doing your "to do" list.
Buying an expensive "to do" list computer
program and never using it.
Finding an old "to do" list and realizing none
of it ever got done.
Others telling you what to do.
"New & Improved" products not as good as
the old versions.
"New & Improved" products claiming to be
better because they've removed all
the preservatives and additives.
"New & Improved" products costing more
because they removed all the stuff
they'd added in the first place.
Getting trapped in the "turn only" lane when
you want to go straight ahead.
Missing your exit on the expressway.
Drivers who back up for missed exits.
Squashing a juicy bug in your favorite book.

You'll never be a famous rock star.
You'll never be a rich rock star.
You'll never have groupies tossing their
        underwear at you from the audience.
Getting a great idea and discovering da
        Vinci got it 500 years ago.
Getting a great idea and discovering
        Maimonides got it 800 years ago.
Getting a great idea and discovering
        Letterman got it last night.

Hairdressers who want to cut your hair their
        way.
Seeing new wrinkles on a friend who's six
        months older than you.
Seeing new wrinkles on a friend who's six
        months younger than you.
Your own new wrinkles.
Not taking a brownie at the buffet table and
        finding they're all gone when you get
        back.
Finding Heaven-knows-whose two-hour calls
        to Upper Peruvia on your long-
        distance phone bill.
People who confuse hearsay with facts.
People who form opinions on hearsay alone.
Thinking up a great comeback an hour after
        you were insulted.

Dead tennis balls.
Tennis rackets with no sweet spot.
Cement-court potholes.
Grass-court stains on your tennis whites.
Sagging nets.

The tennis balls all on one side of the net.
Your forehand smash sending the ball over
        the fence.
Your backhand chop sending the ball into
        the net.
Your cross-court winner sending the ball into
        the next court.
Beginners in the next court hitting tennis
        balls into your court.
Beginners showing up with the latest high-
        tech racquets.
After 50 expensive lessons, getting beaten by
        a friend who "hasn't played in years."
Paying for expensive new-fangled putters
        that don't improve your golf score by
        even one stroke.
Whispering TV golf commentators.
Grown-ups who make crowd noises with
        their mouths.
Grown-ups who make artillery sounds with
        their mouths.
Grown-ups who make rude sounds with
        their armpits.

The smell of gasoline.

The smell of gasoline when you're nowhere near a gas station.

Shopping malls the size of Texas.

Needing a restroom at the far end of a mall the size of Texas.

Hermetically sealed, totally impenetrable potato chip bags.

Opening the bag and finding only potato chip dust.

People who drive exactly 55 mph in the passing lane, just to make a point.

The bottle of correction fluid drying solid.

The correction fluid applicator frizzing into a mascara brush.

Typewriter ribbons running out in mid-page.

Grated Parmesan cheese clumps that rattle in the can but won't shake out.

Plastic punch-out tops on the grated Parmesan cheese that rattle in the can and end up on the linguini.

Having to shave your face every morning.

Having to shave your legs every morning.

Another navy blue tie for Christmas.

Another handmade ashtray for Mother's Day.

Another pen-and-pencil set for graduation.

Another dusting powder set for Grandma's birthday.

People who don't consider the time-zone difference when they call long distance.

Wrapping paper that doesn't fit all the way around the gift.

All the work you put into wrapping a gift that's torn open in three seconds.

Having only baby-shower paper on hand to wrap Uncle Vito's birthday gift.

Diving and scraping your knee on the
bottom of the pool.
Too much chlorine in the pool.
Too many people in the pool.
Too many leaves in the pool.
Pool pee'ers.
Floating algae clots.
Kids cutting into your lane while you're
swimming laps.
Bellyfloppers splashing you while you're
napping in the sun.
Kids shrieking while you're napping in the
sun.
The sun going in just as it gets quiet.
All the good lounge chairs being taken.
Guests who look in your medicine cabinet.
Guests who expect you to be their maid.
Being banished from the nice bathroom
because Mom cleaned it for the
guests.
Guests who actually use the guest towels.
Wiping your hands on your pants because
the guest towels look to pretty to use.
Scratchy bathtowels.
Washed-up washcloths.
Sliding bathmats.
Light too weak to run your solar calculator.
Light too bright to see your digital readout.
Calculator batteries that die just before the
total.
Smart-mouth talking computers.
Cheery wake-up messages from synthesized
digitized voices.
Realizing that systems designed to stop
digital audio bootleggers also keep
you from taping your own CDs.
The black ionized soot that builds up on
TV screens.

Mid-cycle washing machine breakdowns.
"Colorfast" T-shirts bleeding all over white
      loads of clothes.
Spilling bleach on your favorite anything.
Removing what's left of a "dry clean only"
      garment from the washing machine.
Grainy soap clumps on the finished laundry.
No dryers available when your wash is done.

Dryers that eat one sock each load.
Neighbors who take your damp clothes out
      of the apartment house dryer to put
      their stuff in.
Being a quarter short to get your wash
      dried.
Jeans still damp after an hour in the dryer.
Finding faded dollar bill fragments in the
      lint trap.
Canned laughter on bad TV sitcoms.
Finding your favorite TV sitcom cancelled
      after four episodes.
Tacky movies recycled into feeble TV shows.
Jim Nabors' beautiful voice being used for
      Gomer Pyle.
Italian dinners after horror movies.
Jello being more fun to play with than to
      eat.
The strange noise in your car stopping as
      soon as you get it to the shop.

Overblown Superbowl pregame shows.
Overblown Superbowl halftime shows.
Superbowl blowouts.
Sitting in front of ear-splitting whistlers at
ballgames.
Passing hot dogs and money back and forth
for hungry fans down the aisle.
Getting hungry from the hot dogs passing
under your nose, after the vendor's
moved on.
Loud fans who root for the wrong team.
Beer spillers in the row behind you.
Beer spillers on the deck above you.
Beer spillers next to you doing The Wave.
Frisbees clipping you from the blind side.
Getting stomped by fans trying to catch a
foul ball.
Trying to watch sports events sitting next to
people who talk your ear off.
Trying to watch sports events with people
who hate the sport.
The pitcher's salary exceeding the GNP of
many third-world nations.
Softball players with shiny top-of-the line
equipment who can't field or hit.
Being chosen last, for a pick-up softball
game.
Striking out with the bases loaded.
Hitting an easy pop-fly with the bases
loaded.
Dropping an easy pop-fly with the bases
loaded.
Broken glass in the infield.
Broken lights in the outfield.
Broken water fountains in the dugout.
Your muscles, the day after the first game
of the season.
Pete Rose.

"No Vacancy" motel signs late at night, in
the middle of nowhere.
Travelers who pulled in before you and took
the last room.
And the next motel is 60 miles away.
And $60 more.
Non-smoking rooms that reek of cigarettes.
Tiny little motel soaps.
Lumpy mattresses.
Paper-thin pillows.
No-water-pressure showers.
Flimsy locks on motel doors.
Realizing that 600 people could have copies
of your motel-room key.
Itching suddenly after climbing into the bed.
Not being able to figure out how to get an
outside telephone line.
Sleeping through the alarm clock.
Sleeping through the wake-up call.
The motel maid ignoring your "Do Not
Disturb" sign.
Desk clerks who can't give you directions
back to the highway.
Towels that leave fuzz on your stubble.
Hand towels not much bigger than
washcloths.

Bath towels not much bigger than hand
towels.

Passengers who drum on the dashboard.
Passengers who clutch the dashboard.
Passengers who commandeer your radio.
Passengers who rummage through your
glove compartment.
Drivers who turn their cars into rolling
boomboxes.

People who set their packages on your car.
Setting your packages on someone else's car
before you realize the driver's inside,
glaring at you.
Your car stalling as the light turns green.
Learning to drive a stick-shift.
Friends wanting to learn to drive stick-
shifts. On your car.
Riding with someone who can't drive a stick-
shift.
Snifflers who don't blow their noses.
The janitor picking the moment you want to
use the restroom, to clean it.
Not having a quick intelligent response
when someone tries the bathroom
doorknob.
Walking in socks on wet carpeting.
Food that stays on the fork only halfway to
your mouth.
Dropping food in your lap and missing the
napkin.

Your keychain opening in your pocket.
Your keychain opening on the street.
Breaking a nail loading your keys onto a
        new keychain.
Surly waitresses.
Waiters who slam down plates.
Nine-digit zip codes.
Only two clerks for the endless lines at the
        post office.
Fellow airplane passengers who tell you
        their life stories.
Fellow passengers who get airsick.
Motorists who drive away untouched from
        accidents they cause.
Dance partners who never look at you.
Dance partners who sing in your ear.
Off-key.
That faint whiff of gas.
That garbage smell that makes you faint.
Space telescopes that don't focus.
Automatic cameras that won't focus.
Space program projects being built by the
        lowest bidders.
Highway drivers who pace you in your car's
        blind spot.
Jiggly headlights.
Rattling air conditioners.
Untraceable car squeaks.
Turning on the radio at the end of your
        favorite song.
Cranking up the volume and getting a
        barrage of nonstop commercials.
Jokes with endings you can see coming a
        mile away.
Movies with endings you can see coming a
        mile away.
Affairs with endings you can see coming a
        mile away.

Electric sharpeners that devour pencils.

Long sharp pencils with dirty worn-down erasers.

Short chewed pencils with the best erasers.

Needing to copy legal-sized documents with only letter-sized paper.

Copier toner on your clothes.

Finding a business card in your pocket and not remembering why you have it.

Having a business card and not remembering the person you got it from.

Finding a scribbled phone number and not remembering whose it is.

Not being able to find a scribbled phone number.

Left-arm driver's sunburn.

Getting a sunburn from an overcast day.

Peeling off sheets of sunburn.

Realizing you don't have any clean underwear as you dress for work.

Realizing you forgot to use deodorant after you leave for work.

Stale music videos.

Music videos that glorify talentless power-chord teen icons.

Remakes of songs that sound exactly like the originals.

Too much testosterone.

Too little testosterone.

Condoms that fall out of your pocket
prematurely.

Silver-screen heartthrobs losing their hair.

Sex symbols putting on more than a few
pounds.

Finding your side-view mirrors bumped.

Realizing your warranty is void because
your tires have been under-inflated.

Running over large unidentifiable objects in
the road.

Running over large unidentified objects in
the road and dragging them behind
you.

Closing the car door on your seat belt.

Closing the car door on your coat.

Closing the car door on your finger.

Forgetting your gas cap at the station.

Forgetting your briefcase on top of your car
as you drive off.

Forgetting your soft drink on the dashboard
as you make a hard left.

The directions blowing out the window when
you're only half-way there.

Massive warehouse-sized furniture stores
that make you pull your own sofas off
the shelves and onto dollies.

Going into a warehouse-sized furniture store
for a picture frame and coming home
with a five-piece bedroom set.

That you have to assemble yourself.

The touch-up paint for your car never
matching the original color.

That white car wax residue never completely
buffing out of the trim.

Noticing your gauge is on 'E' when you're
late for an appointment.

The moviegoers behind you kicking the back of your seat.

Having to laugh at bad jokes because your boss is telling them.

Not laughing at dirty jokes because it would embarrass your escort.

Not laughing at all in comedy clubs.

Laughing at the wrong point in a joke.

Everybody laughing at you for laughing.

The comedian humiliating you in front of your girlfriend.

The comedian humiliating you in front of a national TV audience.

Shoppers who sneak more than ten items through the express line.

Pairs of fused shopping carts.

Realizing the grocery cart you're pushing isn't yours.

Lazy shoppers leaving their carts alongside your car.

Car door dings from runaway shopping carts.

Not getting enough sleep.

Not getting enough food.

Not getting enough sex.

People who want it all but do nothing to earn it.

People who get it all anyway.

Poor merchandise selection at sales.

Sale-sharks who pounce on what you're eyeing.

Pencil leads that break.

Doggie greetings with muddy paws on your white slacks.

Ripping only three-fifths of the sheet out of a spiral notebook.

People who find fault with everything.

People who can't calculate a 15% tip.

People who tell you how you should spend your money.

People who spend lots of money when you're out of cash.

Toothpaste pumps that don't show they're about to run out.

Roommates who don't tell you they've used up all of your shampoo.

Hiccups.

Strangers who volunteer sure-fire cures for hiccups.

Sure-fire hiccup cures that don't work.

Sneezing fits.

Coughing fits.

Smokers' hacking fits.

People eating faster than you, off a shared plate.

"No pie for me, I'll just taste yours."

Forgetting to turn on the dishwasher.
Forgetting to turn on the answering
         machine.
Forgetting to turn on the burglar alarm.
Forgetting to program the VCR.
Finding out you recorded a one-hour TV
         show with only 40 minutes left on the
         tape.
Taping over the show you meant to watch.

Nosy neighbors with video cameras.
Relatives who won't put down their new
         video cameras.
Being videotaped during an embarrassing
         moment.
Having to relive that embarrassing moment
         at parties.
Having to relive that embarrassing moment
         on a national home-video television
         show.
Book jacket blurbs more exciting than the
         book.
Books with large type and wide margins to
         make them look more expensive.
Books that display the author's name larger
         than the title.
Bookstores that hide promising new books
         on bottom shelves.
Bookstore clerks who never read books.

Bumper stickers that say, "I-HART-N.Y."
Women who apply makeup while they drive.
Men who excavate their noses while they
       drive.
People who cut you off to get the last
       parking spot.
People who don't signal they're not leaving
       until you've waited five minutes for
       their parking space.
Your family will never be anything like
       Father Knows Best.
Your family will never be anything like the
       Waltons.
Your family will never be anything like the
       Huxtables.
Your family may always be more like the
       Simpsons.
Klutzes.
Yutzes.
Putzes.
Teachers who say, "Do you want to share
       that with the entire class?"
Teachers who say, "I know this isn't your
       only class" before heaping tons of
       work on you.
Teachers who say, "There are no stupid
       questions" and then look at the
       ceiling when you ask one.
Students who ask stupid questions just for
       brownie points from the teacher.
Students who never study and get better
       grades than you.
Students who cheat and get better grades
       than you.
People who ask you for the time, all the
       time.
Being called "Guy" or "Buddy."
The smell behind a restaurant.

Hulking 20-year-old trick-or-treaters.
Amateur theater productions of Neil Simon
     plays.
Amateur theater productions of "Evita."
Amateur theater productions of any
     Shakespeare play.
Touring companies of "South Pacific."
The musical segments on the Academy
     Awards show.

Customer service departments that don't.

Programming executives who haven't yet learned that the world doesn't need another late-night talk show.

People who say "irregardless."

People who say "very unique."

People who say, "I could care less" when they mean they couldn't care less.

Your spelling bee wins are so far behind you that you need a dictionary to spell "restaurant."

Your high school Latin classes are so far behind you that you need a dictionary to spell "Caesar Salad."

The hostess seating a family of seven next to your booth.

All of that family's kids being under 12.

Yesterday's lettuce.

Yesterday's take-out egg foo yung.

Yesterday's take-out shrimp in lobster sauce.

Former celebrities now doing supplemental insurance commercials.

Former celebrities now doing denture cream commercials.

Former celebrities now doing adult diaper commercials.

Diarrhea.

Potholes.

Leaving the coupons at home.

Leaving the shopping list at home.

Leaving the checkbook at home.

Office temps with attitudes because they know it's temporary.

Department store Santas who look like skid row regulars.

Holiday-season temps who can't answer questions about the stock or store policies.

Restaurants that serve rock-hard butter on
ice.

Restaurants that warm bread in the
microwave.

Restaurants decorated in "tacky Chinese
bordello" style.

Restaurants decorated in cold bare flat-black
high-tech style.

Plastic lotion tubes that don't show how
much is left.

Smokers who toss lit cigarettes out of car
windows.

Any painting on black velvet.

Men who sit with their knees wide apart on
bench seats next to you.

Armrest turf wars with the guy next to you.

Forgetting birthdays.

Having others remember your birthday
when you forgot theirs.

People who demand to know how old you are
on your birthday.

Rap groups doing Christmas carols.

The year you drop those deadbeats from
your Christmas card list, and they
finally send you a card.

Mimeographed Christmas newsletters.

Not getting mimeo'd Christmas newsletters.

Receiving a more expensive gift than you
gave.

Receive a much cheaper gift than you gave.

Having to care about the cost of gifts you
give.

Flabby kissers.

Sissy kissers.

Sloppy kissers.

Slurpy kissers.

Chew-your-face and take-out-your tonsils
kissers.

Grape-colored hickeys in visible places.
Vitamins that make you pee chartreuse.
Eating more fiber makes more methane.
Cold rainy mornings.
Not enough snow to close the schools, but
    enough to foul up the drive to work.
Hearing that the weather is terrific
    everywhere else.

Commuters who prop up mannequins to use
    rush-hour carpool lanes.
Commuters with car phones who rat on
    carpool-lane violators.
Women with five-inch-long acrylic talons.
Painted black.
With little airbrushed designs on them.
Handling your food in restaurants.
Every 20 years some nauseating new pastel
    color becoming stylish.
People who think they can sing.
People who forget the words to the national
    anthem.
Grown men who refer to grown women as
    "girls."
Paying clerical professionals poorly because
    they're "girls."
Scraping your armpits with the plastic
    applicator when the deodorant stick
    runs out.

Someone else having custody of the TV
        remote control.
Remote controls with no mute.
Losing the remote control.
Losing your slippers.
Losing the good scissors.
Losing the end of the invisible adhesive
        tape.
People who borrow your pen and then chew
        on it.
Cars parked so close to yours that you can't
        open the doors.
Poltergeist seatbelts that jump when you
        close the car door.
Uninsured drivers.
Non-English speaking uninsured drivers.
Commercials trumpeting "the painful itch
        of hemorrhoidal tissue."
Commercials with jerky camera shots.
Feeling your nose starting to run.
Only your cloth napkin in your lap and your
        nose starting to run.
Forgetting to reset the clock for Daylight
        Savings Time.
Forgetting to reset the clock for Standard
        Time.
Having to go through all 23 hours to reset
        the digital clock.
Finding a police boot on your tire.
Finding a police dog on your tire.
Stopping short, holding a cup of coffee.
Very hot coffee in inadequate paper cups.
Trying to hold paper cups full of hot coffee
        by those thin little paper handles.
Overly-sensitive car alarms.
That go off at four in the morning.
And shriek for half an hour.
Discovering it's *your* car alarm.

Kids over 30 who still expect handouts from their parents.

Kids over 30 who still live with their parents.

Paula Abdul not needing you to escort her to the Grammy Awards again this year.

Paul Simon not thinking of bringing you to the Grammy Awards again this year.

Trying to light matches outdoors in the wind.

Squeezing a sneeze.

Squelching a belch.

Gut-wrenching gas pains in a crowded car.

Your hostess's specialty entree looks vile.

Restaurants too dark to read the menu.

Waiters who back away from your table smiling and nodding, but don't write down your order.

Endless pasta.

One measly anchovy in the Caesar Salad.

Snooty maitre d's.

Entrees showing up before the appetizers are finished.

You order rare, you get well-done.

You order well-done, you get bloody rare.

Dribbling on your shirt.

Dribbling on your date.

Dates who dribble on themselves.

Getting shorted on your paycheck.
Getting laid off with the highest references.
Co-workers who polish their nails at their
    desks.
Co-workers who clip their nails at their
    desks.
Co-workers' airborne nail clippings.
Paying for overnight letters that don't arrive
    the next day.
Mail-order gifts that arrive after the
    occasion.

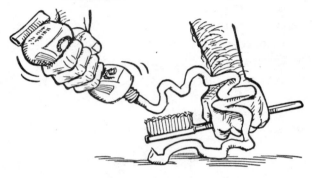

Squeezing out too much toothpaste.
Clogging your toilet.
Clogging a hotel room toilet.
Clogging a friend's toilet.
Leaders who hold meetings while seated on
    the john.
Know-nothings eager to give you directions.
Know-nothings eager to give you stock
    market tips.
Tabloid newspapers.
Inquiring minds that read tabloids at the
    grocery checkout.
But make fun of people who buy them.
Needing an exterminator.
Having to empty out the cupboards for the
    exterminator.
That post-exterminator smell.

The big game being blacked-out at home.

Your favorite player getting traded to the rival team.

Having to stay up till 1 a.m. to see the end of Monday Night Football.

The home team losing to the worst team in the league.

The home team IS the worst team in the league.

Twilight Zone fans who blurt out the ending two seconds into the episode.

People who tell the same tired jokes every time they see you.

People who say, "Stop me if you've heard this one" but don't when you try.

The minute hand obscuring the date on your wristwatch.

Leaks in your grocery bag.

Leaks in your purse.

Leaks in your travel kit.

Missing a connecting flight.

Waiting three hours for the next connecting flight.

People who ask you personal questions during business meetings.

People who base their business decisions on your answers.

Spilling coffee all over your day book.

Spilling coffee all over your desk calendar in January.

Arriving at work with shaving cream behind your ear.

Disappointing prizes in cereal boxes.

Fatal attractions.

Fatal errors.

Fatal femmes.

Buying condoms.

Buying condoms and then not needing them.

Sneezing twice and having to wait for the third one.

Cheap aftershave.

Cheap perfume.

Cheap dates.

Too much salt.

Too much pepper.

Too much curry.

Wet slippery floors.

Waxed slippery floors.

Grayed grout.

Blackened grout.

Missing grout.

Cleaning the bathroom.

Cleaning the microwave.

Records that skip.

Cassettes that unspool.

Compact discs that misfire.

Used CDs costing as much as new ones.

Living too near the airport.

Living too far from the airport.

Co-workers who talk incessantly about their kids.

Co-workers who sell Girl Scout cookies for their kids.

Co-workers whose kids are "The smartest and best at everything, and not just because they're my kids."

The car stereo popping out the cassette and teeth-crunching FM static kicking in.

Designer children's clothing that costs a month's utility payment and is outgrown almost as fast.

Parents who don't strap their children into car seats.

Zig-zagging highway drivers.

Drivers who won't change lanes when you flash your brights.

People who talk babytalk to their cats.
People who have long conversations with
        their dogs.
People who swear at inanimate objects.
Men who name their body parts.
Losing the end of the plastic wrap.
Trying to tear off a narrow strip of
        aluminum foil.
Price tags you can't peel off.
Gummy price tag residue.
The phone ringing and ringing and no one
        answering.
Co-workers who refuse to pick up the phone
        when the receptionist is on break.
Outdoor bank time/temperature signs that
        are off by a few minutes/degrees.
Free estimates that aren't.
No-obligation offers that are.
Chewing your gum too long.
Half-lit neon signs.
Shoppers who munch their way through the
        grocery store.
Shoppers who leave their carts in the middle
        of the aisle.
Shoppers who put unwanted meat and
        frozen food in the magazine racks at
        the checkout.

Dry-mouth smiles that split your lip.
Warmly-signed Christmas cards from people
     you never heard of before.
Last-minute invitations.
Swiping your white shirt with an uncapped
     ballpoint pen.
Swiping your white couch with an uncapped
     felt-tipped marker.
Swiping your boss's white couch with an
     uncapped felt-tipped marker.
Passengers who complain about legroom on
     bench seats in short drivers' cars.
Anything "R" us.
Checkers cheaters.
Scrabble cheaters.
Pictionary cheaters.
Sales on items you just bought at retail.
Bogus "suggested list prices."

Pentagon paying suggested list prices.
Nit pickers.
Bean counters.
Fussbudgets.
Sticklers.
Faultfinders.
Hairsplitters.
Pussyfooters.

Leaving your watch on somebody else's nightstand.

Whom you were not planning to call again.

A third party finding your watch on somebody else's nightstand.

Secret banana bruises that you don't see on the peel.

Rock-hard melons.

Mealy apples.

Tough tomatoes.

More bun than hotdog.

The cereal box rattling, but it's powder and crumbs.

Discovering you're out of milk after the cereal's in the bowl.

Non-stick cookware that does.

Tipsy oil tanker captains.

Loud pendulum clocks.

Realizing you've just said something wrong, seconds before the critics pounce.

People who complain we left out their personal crabbies, but don't send them in to us.

People who laugh out loud reading this in the store and then put it back on the shelf.

People who say "this is perfect for so-and-so" but then wouldn't spring the few bucks to get it for him.

People who fan through a book quickly and then say they don't like it.

Long-lost grade school classmates who resurface to ask for free copies of your book.

Having to choose between looking square or baring all at nude beaches.

Men who only remove their lens caps at nude beaches.

Relatives who still circulate embarrassing pictures from your childhood.

Relatives who bring up embarrassing anecdotes from your childhood.

Everyone thinking they invented parenthood when their first baby comes along.

Trendy names like Rumer, Stradley and Dakota.

Parents who don't discipline their smart-mouth kids.

Visits from in-laws.

Long visits from out-of-town in-laws.

You're always either nostalgic for or sick-to-death of Christmas carols.

Trying to remember all the words to songs you sing only once a year.

Spending a fortune for a winter vacation in the sun, and home had warmer weather that week.

Getting sick right before your vacation.

Drivers who go miles out of their way to save three cents on a gallon of gas.

People who make fun of you for driving out of your way to save money on gas.

Gasoline priced with an extra 9/10ths-of-a-cent, to make each gallon seem a penny cheaper.

Pre-sliced pull-apart English muffins that aren't and don't.

Designer cookies at $11 a pound.

Developing a taste for $11-a-pound designer cookies.

"Homemade" cookies that are perfectly round.

Finding nothing worth eating on a midnight refrigerator raid.

Getting your change in old torn bills.

Getting your change in beer-soaked bills.

Getting your change in singles because the clerk's out of fives.

Getting your change in pennies and nickels because the clerk's out of quarters.

Watches that cost as much as small cars.

Your watch battery dying 45 minutes before an important meeting.

Falling asleep with your mouth open.

Waking up feeling parched and foolish.

The hot water heater picking late Saturday night to die.

The air conditioner picking the Fourth of July weekend to die.

Finding a typo in your resume after you've mailed out 100 copies.

The strap breaking on your shoulder bag.

The handle breaking on your suitcase.

The handle ripping on the garbage bag.

The rental video not being rewound, but you'll be fined if you don't rewind it.

Videos that don't track right.

People who don't know you can fix the tracking by turning a little knob.

Paying extra for "deluxe trail mix" and it's still mostly peanuts and raisins.

Cats that insist on sitting in the middle of whatever you're doing.

People who ask "Are you okay?" and then
      don't listen to the answer.
People who ask if you're okay when you're
      obviously not.
People who defend obvious mistakes.
People who need a reason for everything.
Cat hair.
Dog hair.
Vacuuming cat and dog hair.
Airport cafeteria food.
Airport cafeteria food prices.
Molded plastic scoop chairs with one leg
      broken.
New construction that blocks your view.
That cold-sensitive tooth.
That sweet-sensitive tooth.
That little-ache, soon-to-be-expensive tooth.
Intricate lingerie too much trouble to get
      into and out of.
Bra straps peeking through halter tops.
Being single and getting the flu.
Being married and taking care of a whiny
      mate with the flu.
That scratchiness in your throat before a
      cold.
Coming down with laryngitis right before
      your speech.
Doctors who say "How are we today?"
Nurses who wake you up to take your
      sleeping pills.
Shots.
When the X-ray shows your sprain is really
      a fracture.
Itches under casts.
Point-makers who punch your arm for
      emphasis.
Pets that hate to be petted.
Pets in love with your leg.

New York City streets are always deserted in the movies.

Los Angeles buildings always look cleaner in the movies.

Chicago looks grayer and flatter in the movies.

Washington, D.C. looks more interesting in the movies.

Women wearing ties.

Women wearing scarves that are really just puffy ties.

Clip-on ties.

Chewed-up string ties.

People who repeat themselves.

People who repeat themselves.

Explanations that take twice the time of just doing it yourself.

TV characters always knowing just what to say in awkward situations.

Realizing you're hooked on nasal spray.

Dragging chairs along tile floors.

Dragging fingernails along chalkboards.

Jim Bakker.

Tammy Faye.

Runny mascara.

Clumpy mascara.

Bloodshed in the name of religion.

People who don't flush.

Public toilets that don't flush.

Public restroom stall doors that don't close
completely.

No dividers between urinals.

Troughs.

Pay toilets.

Pay toilets, and no coins.

Restrooms with hot air dryers and no paper
towels.

Restrooms with empty paper seatcover
dispensers.

Toilet paper dispensers that give out one
thin tiny folded sheet at a time.

Toilet paper that doesn't rip at the
perforations.

Guests who use outrageous amounts of toilet
paper.

Finding the toilet paper backwards on the
roller.

Adjusting the toilet paper on the roller the
right way and finding it backwards
again the next time.

Strangers who strike up conversations from
the next bathroom stall.

Finding out too late that your toilet stall is
out of paper.

Mushy overcooked vegetables.
Pistachios that won't open.
Jelly donuts that leak.
Instant gourmet cappuccino.
People who take cordless phones into the
bathroom.
Hearing a flush over the phone.
Being put on speakerphone.
Crackly cellular phone connections.
Blind dates.
Blind dates who sound too good to be true.
Blind dates too stupid to know you're the
best thing that's ever happened to
them.
First-thing-in-the-morning hair.
First-thing-in-the-morning stiffness.
First-thing-in-the-morning mouth.
Bosses who have been with the company
two months but know more than you.
Lackadaisical workers who don't care
enough to do the job right if no one
is watching.
Making office coffee and coming back to
find it already gone.
People who take the last donut and leave
the empty box.
People who straighten things on your desk.
People who leave electric typewriters on
overnight.
People who leave electric blankets on all
day.
Remembering things that never happened.
Fumble-foots who don't say "excuse me."
Fumble-hands who spill things on you at
parties.
Fumble-tongues who take forever to get to
the point.
Trying to hang wallpaper by yourself.

Used gum wads in ashtrays.

Used gum wads in water fountains.

Used gum wads in porcelain conveniences.

Eating two-star meals in four-star restaurants.

Waiters who bring only one glass when you both ask for water.

Bartenders who give you a wedge when you asked for a twist.

Fountain drinks that are 90 percent ice.

Someone else's lipstick on your glass.

Bits of cork floating in your wine.

Waiters who interrupt your dinner jokes at the punchlines.

Dates who order for you without consulting you first.

Dates who order the most expensive things on the menu.

Waiters who make change with fives, to get a bigger tip.

Forgetting your umbrella after leaving a lousy tip.

Forgetting the doggie bag after leaving a good tip.

People in front of you, hesitant to get on the escalator.

People who stop at the bottom of the escalator.

Unattended children running up the down escalator.

Movie-goers leaving the earlier show who give away the ending.

Overhearing someone explain something, loudly and wrong.

Arguments for arguments' sake.

"Wait-persons."

"Fire-persons."

"Postal-persons."

Buying books you never have time to read.
Packing and moving books you never had
time to read.
Videotaping movies you never have time to
watch.
Buying movies on video and never watching
any of them more than twice.
Breaking one glass in a set of eight.
Losing one fork in a service for twelve.
Replacing a broken heel costing more than a
whole new pair of shoes.
Window shades that won't stay down.
Window shades that won't roll back up.

People who put their dogs in the back of
pick-up trucks.
People who put their kids in the back of
pick-up trucks.
People who order you to "chill out."
No-lipped politicians who say, "Read my
lips."
Local TV sportscasters who edit videotape to
make pro athlete heroes look silly.
Having to use port-a-potties baking in the
hot sun.
Friends in bad moods, who don't want to
talk about it.
Friends in bad moods, who DO want to talk
about it.

Double-dip ice cream cones with the mushier scoop on the bottom.

Ice cream that melts faster than you can lick it.

Wearing your fast-melting ice cream.

Frozen yogurt with as many calories as ice cream.

Trying to decide between Swiss Mocha Almond and Rocky Road.

Nose frostbite from leaning over the supermarket ice cream case, trying to choose.

Buying them both.

Eating them both.

Wishing you'd sprung for the gourmet ice cream, after bringing home the generic cheapo stuff.

Scraping an inch of freezerburn off your ice cream to get to the good stuff in the middle of the carton.

Ice cream too hard to scoop.

Wading through a half-inch of soupy ice cream to get to the middle of the carton.

Discovering your roommate already finished off the middle of the carton.

Discovering all the cherries and almonds are on the picture outside the carton.

Realizing the toaster's not plugged in after
waiting five minutes for your muffin.

The cheese on your open-face sandwich
melting all over the bottom of the
toaster oven.

People who "...oh, but first..." interrupt
themselves.

People who "...well, maybe not..." contradict
themselves.

People who "...do I do that?" answer
questions with questions.

People who don't watch PBS.

People who only watch PBS.

People who say with pride, "I don't even own
a television."

Being the oldest person at a Motley Crüe
concert.

Being the youngest person at a Rolling
Stones concert.

Emergency Broadcast System tests
interrupting your favorite radio
programs.

Airlines that give out their schedules to the
minute but deliver to the nearest
hour.

The one that got away.

The best-looking guy at the wedding is the
groom.

The best-looking woman at the wedding is
the bride.

Nobody at the hotspot health club looks like
the hardbodies in their commercials.

Spending more time in line for the
Stairmaster than on it.

Having to pass the bakery and the deli on
the way home from the health club.

Lifetime memberships to health clubs that
go under.

The only available bridge partner is a Life Master.

The only available bridge partner is a beginner.

The only available tennis partner is a seeded player.

The only available tennis partner has a little plastic racket.

The only available golf partner has a two handicap.

The only available golf partner is a duffer.

The only available arm-wrestling challenger is named Bruno.

The only available arm-wrestling challenger is known around as Jasper, The Pencil-Necked Geek.

The only available prom date is so perfect, you feel like the flawed mortal.

The only available prom date is porky Cousin Farley, in from Wisconsin.

The only available mustard is yellow, and you're in the mood for spicy-brown.

The last available blue sling-back mid-heel pump is a half-size too small.

The last available car on the lot with the options you want is baby-doody yellow.

The last available loaf of Italian bread is dented on the end.

The last available not-sickening, not-stupid Valentine has heel marks on the back.

The last available wedding date that you can get the church is Superbowl Sunday.

The last available infant carseat costs three times what you wanted to spend.

The last available baby sitter knows she's the last available baby sitter.

Smelly feet.

White foot powder that shows up on the
dark rug.

The wrong women being great kissers.

The wrong guys being great wage-earners.

Personal daybooks that cost as much as car
payments.

Ordering pepperoni and the guy delivering
anchovies.

Being too hungry to send back the wrong
pizza.

Discovering that "We'll scrape them off" isn't
an adequate solution.

Losing your "Buy 10, Get 1 Free" card with
seven stamps on it.

Your best friend spotting the last elegant
silverwork necklace in the store, at
the same moment you do.

Strangers who make incredibly personal
remarks when you're pregnant.

Strangers who pat your belly, just because
you're pregnant.

Strangers who launch into delivery horror
stories, just because you're pregnant.

Morning sickness.

Not being able to see your feet after your
second trimester.

Renting *Alien* in your last trimester.

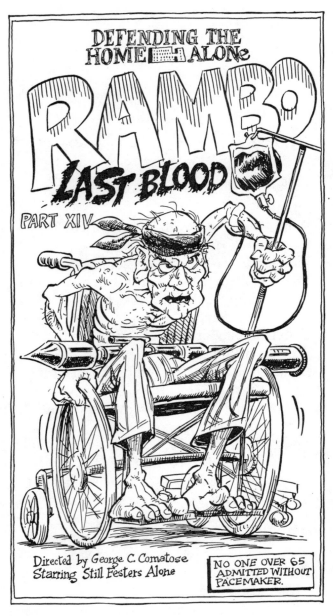

Eternal sequels to Rambo.
Endless sequels to Rocky.
Undying sequels to Freddy.
Unstoppable sequels to Jason.
Inexplicable sequels to Chucky.

Drinkers who insist you join them.

Skiiers who insist you join them.

Skydivers who insist you join them.

People who make a big deal about whether
the restaurant serves Pepsi or Coke.

Discovering you're wearing one black sock
and one blue sock.

No pockets in women's dress suits.

Breaking a pencil point.

Breaking a watchband.

Breaking a bra strap.

Safety pins that open and poke you.

Safety pins that open and poke you during
important meetings.

Yelping for no apparent reason during
important meetings.

Coughers at classical concerts.

People applauding between movements at
classical concerts.

Not knowing when to applaud at classical
concerts.

All your favorite characters leaving your
favorite TV show after the fifth
season.

All your favorite characters getting killed off
on your favorite TV series.

TV series that introduce characters' lovers
and families, just to kill them off
within the hour.

Serial stories that repeat old episodes from
two seasons back.

Seeing one shoe alongside the freeway.

Losing one earring.

Losing one glove.

Not wanting to throw out the mate, in case
you find the first one.

Finding the earring you'd lost after you've
thrown out the mate.

Corned beef on white bread with
   mayonnaise.
Daiquiris made with honey.
Spaghetti and meatballs whose secret
   ingredient is grape jelly.
Escargot eaters who insist on sharing.
Raw oyster eaters who insist on sharing.
Haggis eaters who insist on sharing.
Those chewy onion rings turning out to be
   fried calamari.
The tasteless shrimp crepe turning out to be
   full of snails.
Ordering sweetbreads and discovering it
   isn't sweet and certainly isn't bread.
Fish entrees served with the head on.
Luaus where the entree wears an apple in
   its mouth and an irritated expression
   on its face.
Shellfish dinners you have to execute to eat.
Trying to impress your date in an Italian
   restaurant by ordering Zamboni for
   dessert.
Needing to devour dozens of boring little
   butter cookies to feel like you've had
   dessert.
Knowing the eclairs have gotten a little
   warm, but wanting one anyway.

Tiny ancient drivers behind the wheel.

Not wanting to pass a police car on the highway.

No one else in all four lanes wanting to pass a police car on the highway.

Jammed cruising traffic, at the speed of the police car on the highway.

Kids throwing their old sneakers over the wires in front of your house.

Ripping the sweater you bought two pairs of slacks to match.

Your overworked deodorant insoles curl up and die.

People, who festoon their writing — with: unnecessary punctuation.

People who put "everything in quotation marks."

Being third in line for the john, as the theatre dims the house lights to begin.

Being third in line at the concession stand, and hearing the movie theme music.

Not being able to find your friend saving seats in the dark.

Needing the restroom at the best part of the movie.

Monster trucks on four-foot tires.

Jacked-up trucks with horns that play the first eleven notes of "Dixie."

Car horns that play the theme from The Godfather.

Little burp cars with ARROOGA horns.

Realizing you're working one-third of your life for someone named FICA.

Not being able to deduct credit card interest off your taxes anymore.

Waiters who serve hot salsa and chips but no water to your table.

Pita bread cracking when you try to open it.

People who wouldn't recognize quality if it presented them with an engraved calling card.

The make-up that looked great in your bathroom light looks greenish under the office florescents.

Blind dates you like who don't seem thrilled with you.

Blind dates ready to propose, whom you'd rather never see again.

Wonderful divorcee dates, with horrible kids.

Horrible divorcee dates, with wonderful kids.

First dates who give you big goodnight kisses after not even coming close to you all evening.

Not being able to tell if cantaloupe is ripe before you get it home.

People who are impossible to buy gifts for.

People without the imagination to buy gift certificates for people impossible to buy for.

Having to look pleased and surprised after opening a dumb dud gift.

New Yorker magazine's typeface.

Realizing it's been 25 years since your subscription to *MAD* magazine ran out.

Realizing it's been 15 years since your subscription to National Lampoon ran out.

Realizing you're not getting your issues of Spy magazine because someone keeps lifting them out of your mailbox.

Matchbook covers promising you a new career if you can draw Blinky.

Bus advertising cards promising "u cn gt a gd jb w/gd pay if u cn rd ths."

Having to wear a "HELLO, MY NAME IS
_____" badge.

Discovering you're still wearing your name
   badge hours after you've left the
   meeting.
People who ask your name while you're
   wearing a name badge.
900-numbers promising you can meet great
   new people, who are probably lying as
   much as you are.
900-numbers promising you hot times with
   hot singles at $4.95 per minute.
900-numbers promising you secrets of the
   teen-idol singing stars at $2 per
   minute.
Mommies and daddies receiving phone bills
   for $271 worth of teen-idol secrets.
Roommates demanding details and payment
   for phone bills with $271 worth of hot
   women's confessions calls.
Bathtubs too short to stretch out in.
Trying to blowdry your hair with all the
   shower humidity still hanging in the
   bathroom.
Talking scales that announce your weight
   loudly enough to be heard through
   the bathroom door.
Trying to pull pantyhose onto damp legs.

Not looking enough like your older brother
to use his ID.

Kids who try to use fake ID's.

Trying to find good fake ID's.

Liquor stores that accept fake ID's.

Not being carded anymore.

Independent TV stations running the same
old sitcom episodes over and over.

Cable networks that advertise "30 movies a
month" but run the same five films
six times each.

The movie you've been waiting to see is
running on the cable station at 4:10
a.m. Wednesday.

The movie you've been waiting to see is
running on the one premium cable
channel you don't get.

Cutesy-poopsy "LOVE" stamps.

Bulk mail form-letters promising you can
earn money writing children's stories.

Having to write something down right away,
and scribbling it on the back of
something important.

Finding your kids used the lease as
scribbling paper.

Criminals who make money from books
about their crimes.

People who pay money for those books.

Bumping into your ex's mother on the day
you look hideous.

Bumping into your ex's new spouse on the
day you look ghastly.

Bumping into your ex and the new spouse on
a night when your date is a loser.

Sweaty palms.

Itchy palms.

Rosy palms.

Getting your fingers dirty when you tear up
the carbons from your charge card.

Auto mechanics who test drive your car
without cleaning their hands.

Getting your hands greasy touching the
steering wheel after the mechanic's
test drive.

Writing the last check in your checkbook.

Messing up the last check in your
checkbook.

Having to write checks for less than $10.

Having to write checks for more than $400.

Having to depend on "float" to cover your
checks till payday.

Never being old enough for your mother to
stop wiping smudges off your face in
public.

Former co-workers who say they'll miss you
terribly and then are never heard
from again.

Being fixed up with someone "perfect for
you" because he's breathing and of
your ethnicity.

Being fixed up with someone "perfect for
you" because she's your age and lives
nearby.

Realizing that adorable newly-single guy
won't really be available till he gets
over being dumped.

Calling a co-worker by the wrong name.

Calling a client by the wrong name.

Calling a lover by the wrong name.

Wondering how many years that lone can of
tuna has been in the back of the
cabinet, and is it safe to eat?

Potatoes with eerie sprouting eyes.

Turnips.

Squab.

Finding out what squab is.

Weeds like radicchio suddenly becoming
trendy and expensive.

Housemates who check the phone messages,
and erase them.

Housemates who grab the first shower every
morning.

Housemates who stick you with their long-
distance phone bills.

Housemates who drink milk right out of the
container.

Housemates who leave dishes in the sink.

Housemates who make the house a hostel
for their out-of-town friends.

Insurance salesmen who want to be your
best buddy, until you've signed the
policy.

Insurance claims adjusters who disallow
everything.

Damage estimates only $30 over your
deductible.

The dirtbag bottom-feeding shysters who
call themselves "financial planners"
and spoil it for the real professionals.

"Financial Planners" who use your money to
secure their own financial futures.

Sleazy outcall body-rubbers who spoil it for
legitimate trained licensed massage
therapists.

That pink battery-ad rabbit.

That brown phallic-faced cigarette-smoking camel.

That syrupy-sweet snuggly little teddy bear hawking laundry softener.

That white roly-poly giggly blob of dough that urges you to eat his kin.

Having to be 100 to get a birthday card from the President.

Having to be married 60 years to get mentioned on the Paul Harvey newscast.

Losing 13 pounds without anyone noticing.

Newfangled corkscrews.

Corks that break off in mid-pull.

Bits of cork floating in the wine.

All those pages in your phone bill.

Finding out calls you thought were local are "zone calls," billed at seven cents a minute.

Consolidated multi-account bank statements that confuse you more than three separate statements would.

Having to rotate your food in the microwave.

Rejection.

Rejection letters.

Form rejection letters.

Sunny weekdays with rainy weekends.

Underwear as a gift for any birthday before
you're 18.
The contortions your have to go through to
use that front opening in your briefs.
People who fixate on various parts of your
anatomy when they talk to you.
Uneven ratios at singles dances.
Knuckle crackers.
Shoulder pads in both your blouse and
jacket, giving you that halfback look.

Migrating shoulder pads.
Dry cleaners who pucker shoulder pads.
Paying more to taper your flared trousers
than to buy new pants.
That mother-and-daughter reunion
commercial where they speak so
tenderly about ... douches.
That disposable diaper commercial
promising to stop "messy B.M. leaks,"
running during dinner hour.
Intermission at a 500-seat theater with only
three stalls in the ladies room.
All the restroom stalls being occupied.
People who look under the stall door to see if
anyone's in there.
The surfaces Post-it notes won't stick to.
Beauty queens who wear petroleum jelly on
their teeth.

Sneaker squeaks on basketball courts.

The last five minutes of a game taking half an hour.

Your team getting trounced in overtime.

Cutting to a commercial at the last second of a boxing round.

Choreographed professional wrestling.

Professional wrestlers who scream death threats into the microphone during their interviews.

Sports-stars turned sports-commentators turned hardware-store-hawkers.

Finding out your expensive new company letterhead won't go through the expensive new laser printer.

Finding someone left the good letterhead in the copier paper tray after you've run off 30 copies of a recipe.

Placing the original on the copier glass the wrong way.

"The computer's down."

Cassette tapes that you can't splice when they break.

Cutting your tongue licking an envelope.

Plasticized junk mail you can't tear up.

Those pull-apart envelopes that never do.

The smell of oven cleaner.

Having to clean the self-cleaning oven.

Having to defrost the frost-free freezer.

TV commercials that make you hungry, even though you just ate.

Fast food on TV that never looks like what you get.

People who say "It's not the money, it's the principle," when it's really the money.

People who finish your sentences for you.

People whose speech trails off, so you want to finish their sentences.

Cold stethoscopes.

People who constantly call their message machines.

People who empty their ashtrays in parking lots.

People who buy riding mowers for property less than a quarter-acre.

Starting a vegetable garden and finding your backyard is clay and gravel.

Hitting a boulder two inches below the surface.

Slicing a phone cable ten inches below the surface.

Forgetting which vegetables you planted in which row.

Neighborhood kids using your garden as a shortcut.

The whole neighborhood using your garden as a free produce stand.

Telephone solicitations for your alumni association, made from telemarketing boiler rooms in Nebraska.

Breathy alumni newsletters full of chatter about people you don't know.

Groups you never heard of selling millions of records to people born since you graduated from high school.

Finding out that "thirty minutes of free long distance calling" is worth about three dollars.

Realizing you're listening to someone's accent, and missing everything that's being said.

Finding out cauliflower au gratin still tastes like cauliflower.

Finding out *paté de foie gras* is only fatty chopped liver.

Shoelaces that won't stay tied.

Being made to sit in the first seat on the rollercoaster.

Sitting next to a wuss on the rollercoaster.

Sitting behind someone with a weak stomach on the rollercoaster.

There are no sure bets at the races.

There are no sure bets in the stockmarket.

There are no sure bets in the dating game.

Not being able to wake up from a nightmare.

Dreaming about having to go to the bathroom.

Having to get out of a warm bed to go to the bathroom.

Cold toilet seats.

Toilet seats still warm from the previous user.

Paperboys who throw papers in the bushes.
Paperboys who throw papers on the roof.

Paperboys who throw papers into puddles.
Dogs that wait for paperboys.
Forgetting the number to your combination
     lock.
Mergers and acquisitions making it
     impossible to know who owns what
     anymore.
Even after paying the fines, Michael Milken
     still having more money than Uncle
     Sam.
Incredible department store sales right after
     you've paid off your charge card.
Garage-sale organizers who won't dicker on
     prices.
People who shave messages into the sides of
     their heads.
Women's hairstyles that shave the backs of
     their necks.
Tarnish on your brass.
Tarnish on your sterling silver.
Tarnish on your guacamole.
That smell in nursing homes.
Sunday morning TV being nothing but half-
     hour commercials, faith-healers,
     talking heads, silly cartoons and
     reruns of *The Munsters.*

Forgetting the bug spray on camping trips.
The water tasting funny.
Thinking everything is poison ivy.
Not recognizing real poison ivy.
The tent not looking anything like the
        picture in the catalog.
Camping with people who don't do much at
        home, and do even less in the woods.
Wet firewood.
Wet matches.
Wet toilet paper.
Hearing strange noises right outside your
        tent.
Buzzing little no-see-um bugs right outside
        your ear.
Realizing you've wiggled the sleeping bag off
        the tarp.
Needing to go to the bathroom at 4 a.m.
Realizing where the bathroom is at 4 a.m.
Having to unzip the warm sleeping bag and
        put on your shoes at 4 a.m.
Having left the flashlight on all night.
The lantern not lighting.
Squatting in the woods.
Realizing you actually miss the concrete
        urban setting you're trying to get
        away from.

NO BILLS
SMALLER THAN
$20
ACCEPTED.

Beggars too upscale for pocket change.

Testy people who get testier when you
suggest they're acting testy.

So-called dinner parties that serve cold cuts
and fruit punch.

Watered-down drinks.

Bartenders who won't give you a free drink
after your fourth round.

Pay phones so close together you can't hear
your own conversation.

Paying for home delivery and not getting
your newspapers regularly.

People who talk back to the movie.

People who dare to shush you when you talk
back to the movie.

People behind you asking each other obvious
questions.

Big-haired people in front of you blocking
the screen.

Tall people in front of you shifting in their
seats.

The empty seat in front of you getting taken
just as the movie starts.

People who squeeze past you during the
movie.

People who stand up after the movie and
block the credits.

Digital watch alarms that go off during the
movie.

Strangers who look over your shoulder at
automatic teller machines.

The 24-hour ATM being closed.

The 24-hour ATM being out of cash.

The 24-hour ATM not recognizing your
secret code number.

The 24-hour ATM eating your card.

Tomato slices falling out of your sandwich.

Tomato slices with hard chewy cores.

No one telling you about the glob of
mayonnaise on your chin.

People who are too neat.

People who are too cluttered.

People who pick up after you.

People who won't pick up after you.

Inhospitable nurses.

Having to vote for judges you don't know a
darned thing about.

Dialing a wrong number and getting an
earful of fax machine squeal.

People who'd violate the copyright laws of
this proud country, The United States
of America, by illegally photocopying
any part of this fully protected
registered document on the office
copier.

People who'd count all 1,000,001 of these
things.

HEY!

You left out the one thing that really sticks in my craw!

Next time you write a book about the things that make people crabby, be sure to include:

_____

_____

_____

_____

_____

_____

Have a nice day!

_____
Name

_____
Address

_____
City/State/Zip

Mail your crabbies to:

CorkScrew Press, 4470-107 Sunset Blvd.
Suite 234, Los Angeles, CA 90027

173

HEY!

You left out the one thing that really sticks in my craw!

Next time you write a book about the things that make people crabby, be sure to include:

_____

_____

_____

_____

_____

_____

Have a nice day!

_____
Name

_____
Address

_____
City/State/Zip

Mail your crabbies to:

CorkScrew Press, 4470-107 Sunset Blvd.
Suite 234, Los Angeles, CA 90027

Who *is* this woman?

You can hear Natalie Windsor on the radio in Los Angeles. She's been a local radio news anchor in Cleveland, Rochester NY, Chicago, Phoenix, Los Angeles, and nationally for the Transtar Radio Network.

What Natalie does in her spare time would fry any couch potato. Her resume includes acting in touring repertory theatre; singing professionally in clubs, religious settings of almost every denomination, and Dodger Stadium; volunteer work as a para-chaplain, and a counselor on the *Los Angeles Sex Information Helpline.* She's recorded books on Buddhism and gene-splicing for the Library of Congress Talking Book Program, and is oddly proud of being a past national president of the Committee to End Pay Toilets in America (CEPTIA).

People who turn to the last page first.